American Yellow

by
George Omi

American Yellow
Copyright ©2016 George Omi

ISBN 978-1506-902-22-7 PRINT

LCCN 2016941277

May 2016

Published and Distributed by
First Edition Design Publishing, Inc.
P.O. Box 20217, Sarasota, FL 34276-3217
www.firsteditiondesignpublishing.com

Cover Design: Geoff Omi
Editor: Rosie Narasaki

This book is dedicated to:

Kiyo, my loving wife, my conscience, my guiding light.

Jeanette, my sister, lifelong friend and confidante.

Willie Lang, my loyal friend and a most humble and genuinely gentle man.

Acknowledgements

Jeanette (*Shii-chan*) for letting me tell my story.

Kiyo for her support and help.

Brian, Toshiko, and Garrett for their support and. especially Garrett, for his insightful reading.

Laura, Miyo, Sharon, Grant and Grace for reading my draft and for their helpful comments and encouragement.

And last, but not least, thank you Geoff, and Rosie, for helping me make my story into a book.

Figure 1 *Mama, Shii-chan, Papa, Minoru*

Chapter One

Safety Cleaners
San Francisco, California
December 7, 1941

My sister *Shii-chan* was on the floor, hogging the funny papers like always.

"Will you hurry with that?" I said impatiently.

She had the page with the Katzenjammer Kids. Now that she knew I wanted it, she made me wait. I pretended not to care, but I wanted to snatch it away. But if I did, I might be sorry, so I let it go. Once she got so mad she threw an empty jar of Pond's vanishing cream at me. The jar missed me but shattered the vase on the coffee table. Papa shouted at her in Japanese. When she wouldn't stop sobbing, I'd felt guilty. "It was my fault," I said weakly, but Papa wouldn't listen.

Mama was in the kitchen making breakfast while Papa gargled in the bathroom. He'd been out late with *Rok-san*, his brother, and a few of their friends who had come to America together on the Persia Maru in 1917.

He woke me up last night when he closed the squeaky front door.

I opened my bedroom door slightly to peek, and in the darkness, heard Papa stumble on a foot stool and hit his head on the mahogany table.

"*Ah-h, itai! Ouch*, that hurts," he said. He reeked like the inside of a tavern.

Moments later, when I saw the sliver of light under the bathroom door and heard him vomit, I returned to my bunk bed, slid under the covers, and pulled the pillow over my ears. By the time he came out of the bathroom, I was asleep.

Shii-chan was still pretending to read, so I crawled to the radio and turned it on. With thirteen tubes, the Gilfillan took several minutes to warm up. Finally, the announcer's voice came on faintly, then louder. Darn! The news! I wanted music. I turned the dial, but stopped when I heard "Japanese planes have dropped bombs on the Hawaiian Islands," the announcer's voice said, frantically, "I repeat . .. Japanese aircraft have dropped bombs on the Hawaiian Islands!"

Quickly, I turned up the sound. "Too loud!" my sister yelled.

". . . a heavy attack by Japanese aircraft has destroyed . . . " The voice blared into our living room.

"Too loud!" Papa yelled from the bathroom.

"Come here!" I yelled, "Hurry up and listen!"

"*Urusai, naa*," he complained, "What a pest!" Sleepy eyed, unshaven, Papa shuffled into the room in his underwear, balancing a checkered ice bag on his head. As he listened, his eyes grew larger. Setting the ice bag on the table, he shuffled to the radio and placed his ear near the speaker. He turned the volume down and moved the dial from one station to another. As we listened to the same words, the same frantic voices, over and over, Mama stood silently in the kitchen doorway, wiping her hands on her apron.

No matter what station Papa turned to, the news was the same: The U.S. fleet at Pearl Harbor had been destroyed. Battleships and aircraft carriers had been sunk, confusion; fire and smoke were everywhere. Papa sat by the radio late into the night. I had never seen him sitting that quietly before. Soon, the phone rang: Uncles, aunts, friends -- our whole Japanese community called us.

"*Soh yo*," Papa said over and over in Japanese, "It's their fault for helping the Chinese.

"*Soh...* California, *ka mo shiren*," he said, "California may be next. .."

He began speaking loudly in Japanese. "No! No soldiers in Hawaii, only bombs..." He paused. "I know we're Japanese, I know . . ." His voice grew soft. Finally, he said abruptly, "I have a headache, I'll call you later. " He put the phone down and disappeared into the bathroom until the ringing began again.

Mama watched silently while Papa sat by the radio, turning the dial. It was as if she had lost her power to speak. *Shii-chan* and I sat on the floor pretending to play jacks, our eyes going from one to the other, waiting for life to resume its familiar routine, whispering the questions we didn't dare ask: Would we go to school in the morning? If so, what would our classmates be thinking? What would our teachers say? Are we safe in this neighborhood?

I heard Papa say that President Roosevelt was going to speak tomorrow. He also said that he heard that Japanese soldiers might invade California. What then? I thought. What would become of us? Whose side were we supposed to be on? Such questions rang in my ears. Our world inside the larger world of America was suddenly not safe anymore.

Chapter Two

On that day when Japan bombed Pearl Harbor, Papa had already lived in America for twenty-five years, but he still felt uneasy among *Hakujin*s, or Caucasians. "Too much pressure," he would say. "*Hakujin*, all the time, say, no do this, no do that. No can do nothing. *Hakujin*s no like Japanese. I no can naturalize. I live this country longer than Japan, and I no can buy property in California because I not citizen. Government stop immigration in 1924. You know why? They scare. Japanese work too hard. *Hakujin* get jealousy. They too lazy."

"When I come America in 1917, I go restaurant in Petaluma. *Hakujin* lady get mad. She shout. I no know what she saying. She point finger at door. Everyone laughing. I so embarrassing. I get out, but no go inside *Hakujin* restaurant no more."

With the bombing, our situation had worsened. Suddenly, we were in the limelight without a place to hide; we couldn't change the way we looked. The war made headlines every day, and the radio announced invasions. Newsreels confirmed what the newspapers and radio said.

In school, I felt self-conscious. I was *Nisei*, born of immigrant parents. As a child, I saw how different we were. When I saw *Hakujin*s in the movies, how they lived, and heard them on the radio, I understood what Papa meant. Their world surrounded us, yet was far away. How could we ever become a part of it?

I didn't want to live in Japan, though at times, it seemed inevitable. After school, while my *Hakujin* schoolmates played, I boarded a bus that took me to school in Japanese Town. "Why do I have to go to Japanese School?" I asked one day.

"Someday we go Japan," Papa said with a smile, while ironing a shirt in our cleaners. "You go school, you learn how writing. You writing letter to you grandfather in Japan, I be proud. Maybe you reading Japanese newspaper someday. I be very proud."

"Why would I want to know how to read a Japanese newspaper?" I asked, creasing a sheet of paper for an airplane, "I'm more American than Japanese." I folded the wings.

"You look in mirror. No can change face."

"My third grade teacher said that America is a melting pot."

"She *Hakujin*. She no know."

"But we don't want to live in Japan. . ." *Shii-chan* whined.

Papa pretended not to hear her. "When we have money," he said, "We go. When you big boy and *Shii-chan* big girl, maybe you help . . ." He hung a shirt on a hanger and placed it on a rack.

"Geez, that's a long time from now," I said.

"Maybe go sooner, if lucky."

"Which do you like better?" I said, getting ready to toss the airplane. "Japan or America?" I always got around to asking that question and Papa's answer never changed.

"Japan, where I born. Me, Mama, you, *Shii-chan*, pure Japanese. No mix blood. We many, many generation. Japan very old, more than 2000 years. America young. No history like China or Japan," he said, emphatically, pulling a coat out of the hamper.

The airplane looped and landed under the table. Papa picked it up, put an extra crease in the wings and tossed it toward the counter. This time it nose-dived and he laughed. After we'd folded several airplanes and tossed them around the work area, Papa went back to the pressing machine and I went into the kitchen, where Mama was bent over the sink.

"Why do we have to go to Japanese School?" I asked again.

"Someday you will be glad that you learned the language," she said in her high voice.

"Do you think we'll ever go to Japan?"

"No . . . America is our home. I don't think Papa really wants to go back. He only talks like that. Life is much harder over there."

Chapter Three

Until that fateful Sunday morning, we had our own safe world; despite the uncertainties that surrounded us. I loved Sunday mornings, when the store was closed and without the smell of steam or musty garments. From the kitchen came smells of toasting bread, sounds of crackling bacon, eggs frying, the soft rattling of pots and pans, Mama running water in the sink.

Our cleaners was near the middle of the block between a diner and a welding shop. "New City Cleaners," Papa would tell people proudly, "No can miss. Big neon sign in front." The sign was like magic. It hung over the entrance, softly, glowing, like a misty green fireball. At night the light came off the glass in a green haze, overlaying a cardboard poster of a svelte blonde woman in a satin gown, and a stylish blue-eyed man in a Stetson hat.

New City Cleaners. The words shimmered backwards. If I stood beneath the sign, I could hear it buzzing like so many bees. The minute I saw it, I knew we were home and I felt warm inside. When Papa saw my excitement, he would laugh. "Good for business, that's why I leave on," he would say, but I knew he didn't get it.

New City Cleaners: a cocoon, in which we ate, slept, worked and played. Our world, our territory, our safe haven. It began at the front counter with a sign that said "Employees only," and continued beyond the pressing machine to a high-ceilinged hallway, past stairs to a room cluttered with tables, chairs, and a springy green sofa.

Papa would let no one past the counter except friends. He would point at the sign with his whisk broom and say, "You stay. I get for you."

Beyond the counter, within the work area, I spent most of my early life after school watching Papa work. He brushed each garment carefully with his whisk broom and smoothed out the wrinkles. Then, from his rear pocket he would pull out a white handkerchief, shake it open, and wipe his forehead. Carefully, he would fold it and replace it in his pocket. Then, he would grip the wooden rail attached to the steam head, a large anvil filled with tiny holes, and with his right foot, step down hard to lower the anvil over the garment. When he depressed a lever with his index finger, steam from the anvil made a sizzling sound. Rocking back and forth, he would shift his foot from the center to the right pedal and the machine would roar. I never tired of watching him. If I closed my eyes, I could see his every movement, never changing, like Papa himself.

From within our cocoon, we often heard the clatter of dishes and saucers from the diner next door and the ear-splitting screech of metal against stone from the welders on the other side. These sounds would frequently combine with the familiar sounds of Papa's press machine, the p-s-s-s-t of steam, followed by a roar, and from Mama's Singer sewing machine: a smooth, soft, purr, a quick rat-a-tat, as Mama, pins pursed between her lips, pressed the pedal.

In our cocoon, other senses stirred. Often on a Saturday afternoon the smells of Mama's tempura and teriyaki chicken would mingle with the smell of hot beef sandwiches and coffee from the diner next door. But sometimes these smells succumbed to an offensive garment steaming on the pressing machine. Papa would stand back to avoid the steam, and fan his face while holding his nose. He would point at a garment with his whiskbroom, its empty sleeve dangling across the padded anvil.

"*U-wahhh, kusai*" he would complain, "It stinks!"

I knew the inside of our cleaners as well as the mice that drove Mama near crazy: every crack, crevice; downstairs, upstairs; front and back. In the living room downstairs, I slept with Papa in a bed that disappeared into the wall; Mama and *Shii-chan* slept upstairs in the attic. I often heard Papa and uncle *Rok-san*'s songs, their jokes, their drunken laughter. During the day, I played on the steps that went up to Mama's room, or hid behind the kitchen door, or inside the hall closet where I often heard more than I was supposed to: mostly idle gossip, like how the cobbler's wife, Mrs. Sato, would flirt with *Rok-san* whenever he took shoes into the shop. "It's nothing serious," *Rok-san* would laugh. "She treats all men that way."

"She has eyes for you," Papa would say, "You'd better find another store or else buy another pair when the old ones wear out." Then they both would laugh.

Papa and *Rok-san* bought the cleaners in 1927, a year before Papa married Mama. I was born in 1930, and, my sister in 1932, so we grew up during the Depression. "Business much better before you born," Papa would say, but it had actually been worse. After the stock market crashed in 1929, many garments gathered dust, unclaimed by owners. Such a waste. But while I was growing up, they made neat hiding places. My sister couldn't find me. I'd hide between suits, dresses, and overcoats that hung in double rows on pipe racks, or on the floor against the wall between dusty paper-wrapped bundles filled with unclaimed shirts, sheets and pillow cases. But I was allergic to dust. Sooner or later I gave myself away in a fit of sneezing.

Papa didn't sell the unclaimed garments; instead, he donated them to the Salvation Army. "They very good to me and *Rok-san* when we come to America," he said. Then, to get new business, he cut prices and gave away services. "Business get better, you see," he would say to Mama in Japanese. She would agree, while shaking her head no, in the confounding Japanese manner when no means yes.

Gradually, the dust would accumulate again.

Chapter Four

After President Roosevelt's speech, Papa said, "*U-u-wahh*, this big war.

Japanese navy go everywhere in Pacific Ocean. Philippine, Guam, Malaysia. American navy, no more battleship, I think. *Sohhh . . .*" he thought for a while, "He make good speech. He smart. He mad, but no get mad. I think very hard win with no navy, but he say America win anyway."

Papa, during the days that followed the attack, would huddle near the radio and listen for news, switching the knob from American broadcasts to short-wave. The Japanese stations were elusive. Our living room would fill with static. While this was happening, I'd leave the room and go upstairs.

"Who should we be for?" *Shii-chan* would ask.

"I don't know, but I hope we don't have to go to Japan."

"Me neither," she would say.

We knew we were Japanese. We'd learned their customs, spoke their language, went to Japanese school, and ate with chopsticks. But we were Americans too. We said the "Pledge of Allegiance" in our classroom, sang the "Star Spangled Banner," played cowboys and Indians, and listened to "Captain Midnight" and "Little Orphan Annie" on the radio.

Even Papa loved Joe Louis fights. He'd listen to them on the radio. He also took us to see Bogart movies, and tuned in to the San Francisco Seals baseball team on the car radio. Mama taught us to play jacks, hopscotch and jump rope. She baked a turkey on

Thanksgiving and served it with stuffing, cranberry sauce, and pumpkin pie. In a way, we were an all-American family.

But our cocoon kept us separate -- our language, our food, our music; our Japanese relatives and friends. Yet, oddly, *Shii-chan* and I had never been to Japan. We'd never met our Japanese grandparents, uncles, aunts and cousins. Papa had pointed them out in the photo album and told us their names, and, though he had done this often, the images in the black and white photographs didn't seem real. Without knowing it, we had somehow become misfit Japanese with American minds.

Papa, on the other hand, had a Japanese mind. He grew up in Japan and had come to America innately Japanese. He had known of Western customs, known that Americans wore shoes in their homes, sat in chairs instead of on mats, and ate with silverware instead of chopsticks. He had anticipated these differences before coming to America, but wasn't prepared for the way Americans treated the Japanese. He was unprepared for the discourtesies. The insults came in many forms: polite refusals, to surreptitious profanities, to blatant name-calling.

He came to despise his persecutors. His back would cinch at the word Jap. How he hated its sound on harsh Caucasian tongues. It often came without provocation, was shouted with so much hatred. Why? He had not committed a crime. Why did they snarl and shout angrily at him and his friends? Predators, he thought, animals – smelly and hairy.

Papa spoke in a loud voice, as though shouting would make a difference in America. Everyone delighted in his enthusiastic demeanor. He'd shake hands as though it were for the first time. But his gregarious manner was deceiving. He couldn't take a joke, not even a casual reference or an unintended pun. "Why you call me Shorty?" he would shout angrily at a salesman. "I no like. You get out!"

"I didn't call you Shorty, Mr. *Omi*. I only said that most Japanese are short compared to Europeans. I'm sorry if that offended you." Papa cursed the man in Japanese and went back to work; the salesman snapped shut the locks on his suitcase, and left the store, red-faced.

But Papa also conversed congenially with *Hakujin*s who came into our store. He frequently spoke to shop owners, car mechanics and bankers, and often said things about money that I didn't understand: deposits, withdrawals and accounts.

"Yes, Mr. *Omi*, I know what you mean," they would reply. Papa loved business. "In business," Papa would laugh, "Money talks." He bargained with vendors and brought their prices down. He wrote checks carefully and checked his arithmetic on scratch paper before he penned them into the book. He was proud of his shrewdness.

Papa had wanted an education. "If I in Japan, I college educated," he would say. He'd felt cheated. His father had taken him out of school at fifteen, and summoned him to America to help his brother with a chicken ranch. And then he was conscripted to an apple dryer in Sebastopol for five years. "For what?" he would ask. "My father never let me go back to school, and I never saw the money I earned."

In 1923, after years of cleaning chicken coops and coring apples, Papa had returned to Japan with expectations of wealth, women and an education. His father had invested his money in a poultry business in Yokohama. But a year later, Yokohama was flattened in an earthquake -- burned to the ground. What few chickens that survived the disaster were given away by his father to help feed his friends and neighbors. All of Papa's hard-earned money had literally gone up in smoke. And the land couldn't be sold because no one had any money. There was nothing left for Papa in Japan. In the aftermath, all he had was misery. If nothing else, at least in America, he could find work. And so he returned in 1924 before the immigration law, which would have precluded his return, was passed.

Papa's return was timely. America was prosperous in the '20s, so Papa quickly made up the money he lost. And he enjoyed the freedom from his family's misery. *Hakujins* didn't care what he did, as long as he stayed clear of them. And within the Japanese community he could almost live as he pleased. When he married and had children, he'd felt lucky beyond his dreams. Luckier than his brothers in Japan. Someday he'd show them what luck in America had brought him. Someday, he would take them to the fanciest bars and Geisha houses in Tokyo. "Someday . . ." he would always say to *Rok-san* while they drank at the Nippon Bar and Grill.

Papa may have despised *Hakujins*, for the way they taunted him, but he respected their authority. "America is theirs," he would say in

Japanese. "We are their guests. If this were Japan, I'd treat them the same way."

Papa and Mama had few *Hakujin* friends and I would often ask him why (even though I knew why not). Whenever I asked how many *Hakujin* friends he had, Papa would say, "Not a one."

"Not even after twenty years?" I would say.

"I no like them and they no like me. We no same."

Certainly that was true of the *Hakujin* who rented a room next-door from our cleaners. He was mean. I was in the first grade when I first saw him in the yard. He had come near me with a garden hose. "Stand back," he said, in a gruff voice, dragging the hose to where the flowers were planted. I went back inside and waited until he was through before going back out to the yard.

I eventually learned his name, Mr. Richmond. He worked at night and slept during the day. Sometimes on Saturday afternoons, he would putter about the yard. I tried to be friendly. Once, I went up to him and said, in my friendliest voice, "Good Morning, Mr. Richmond. Nice day isn't it?" But when he could only manage a loud grunt and a scowl, I avoided him thereafter.

I often played alone in the yard. I loved to watch butterflies. Monarchs were my favorite. They would alight softly on Mama's morning glories, opening and closing their wings like soft silk tissue, orange and black, sometimes flying close to an insect I despised. From its head grew strange spherical eyes; it had a dark, thin body with a stinger-like tail. Darting about like a hummingbird, it would fly out of the yard as quickly as it had flown in – the sinister dragonfly.

Mr. Richmond had trouble sleeping during the day. He'd often shout out his window, "Mr. *Omi*, can you keep it quiet down there? I'm trying to sleep." Papa would try to quiet his activity, saw cutting or hammering, and calmly say, "I no like him. Why he no find work like everybody else? He all the time sleeping."

Mr. Richmond was usually asleep when Papa brought live chickens home from Petaluma. When I heard them pecking and cawing, I could hardly wait. I'd forget how they smelled, and stick my head inside Papa's Studebaker sedan. When I came back out holding my nose, Papa would laugh. "See. . . I told you," he would say in Japanese.

I'd watch Papa carry the crates to the side yard and set them down on the cement. Then he would go inside and come out in an apron. With his hammer, he would pry and pry, while looking up at Mr. Richmond's window and the nails would screech. He would pull away the boards, reach in, and grab a frightened hen by its wings. Wild eyed, it would shriek, "Ku-kwraw, ku-kwraw, ku-kwraw." Her head would twist and turn, and the red pouch beneath her bill would keep flapping like a flag. Then he would set her free. Unwrapping her wings, she would strut about the yard, filling the air with her sweet smell -- small, white feathers would follow her like a cloud of dandelions.

While the hens pecked and cawed about the yard, Mr. Richmond would holler, "Mr. *Omi*, would you please do something about your chickens! I can't sleep!"

Finally, Papa would come out to the yard with a cleaver. One by one, he would catch them, and one by one, he would take them to the table, where they screeched and squawked. Then with his glistening cleaver, he slit their throats and suddenly the frightened hens became forever still.

I'd close my eyes and hear the parts fall with a "Shush, shush, shush" into a paper bag -- heads, liver, intestines, and all. When I opened my eyes, I would see his gloves, knife, apron spattered with blood -- its smell was everywhere. And a sickly silence filled the air.

"Why don't you buy them at the store?" I would ask.

"No taste good from grocery store."

That night, I could not even look at Mama's teriyaki chicken.

One cold and foggy San Francisco morning, Mr. Richmond was pulling weeds out of his flowerbed. Dragonflies hovered like gnats around his head, but he paid them no mind. I admired him for that. I wanted to know his secret. I approached him with a watchful eye. "Where do the dragonflies come from, Mr. Richmond?" I asked.

He jumped slightly. "Don't come sneaking up on me that way," he said -- he never called me by name. He must have detected my apprehension, because then he said, "Do you really want to know, boy?" Before I could say no, he plopped down his sack. "I'll tell you what I know for a fact, boy, dragonflies don't like Chinee boys and girls. They come from China like the Chinee dragon. They was brought in by Chinee to help find gold in California. They was supposed to be like bloodhounds that could sniff down animals. Only problem was when they let them out of their cages, they flew away."

He drew closer to me. "In China, they attack schools and chil'run. They get inside your ears and sew inside them until you can't hear no more. When you can't hear no more, you can't talk no more. So when you see these varmints, best you stay inside. "Remember, boy. Don't come out here. Stay inside. And tell your little sister what I said." He picked up his sack and began pulling weeds again. "Stay inside," he mumbled. "Don't be coming out here, again."

Later, when Mama asked me what Mr. Richmond had said to me, I just said that he told me a story about dragonflies, since I didn't want her to tell Papa what he really said.

"What's wrong with that?" she asked.

"He thought we were Chinese."

"Oh . . .?" Mama said just as a customer walked into the store. When she went to the counter, I hurried out to the playground.

I never told Papa how Mr. Richmond had scared me that day. But I knew what he would have said: *Gaman-shite!* "Bear the pain."

Chapter Five

Mr. Goldberg owned the diner next door. He was Jewish. Mama said he was a gentleman. Papa liked him too. I thought he had the heart of Geppetto, the doll maker in "Pinocchio"--- except he looked more like Doc in "Snow White and the Seven Dwarfs." Like Doc, he had a shiny face and round nose. His blue eyes twinkled. Above his ears and below his crown he had a thick thatch of silver hair, but the top of his head was bare. In the mornings when he hadn't shaved, a stubble shadowed his face. If we saw him like that, he would apologize to Mama. "I'm sorry for the way I look, Mrs. *Omi*. I didn't have time to shave this morning."

I overheard Mr. Goldberg tell Mama, "If I ever hear my tenant, Mr. Richmond, talk that way to your son again, Mrs. *Omi*, believe me, I will ask him to leave. The nerve of that man. Dragonflies, indeed!"

After school, I would stand in front of Mr. Goldberg's diner and smell the bread baking in his oven. When he wasn't busy with diners, I'd go inside, sit on a stool, and spin the one next to it. He would smile, set a glass on the counter, and pour milk into it. Then he'd put a donut on a plate and hand it to me with a napkin.

He worked behind the counter in an aisle. Behind him, against the wall, was his work table, stove, griddle, ice box, and sink. He kept dishes, mugs, and glasses under the counter and pots, pans on hooks above his work table. He would talk to me over the counter, while wiping it with a towel. Mrs. Goldberg died in an automobile accident, he'd said. Though he didn't have children of his own, he said he had a nephew in Scarsdale, New York, "He's about your age," he told me, while removing my empty glass from the counter.

Mr. Goldberg opened his diner every morning at six, and closed it at three in the afternoon. Most all his customers lived or worked nearby. Men from the welding shop would come in with dirty faces, in grease spotted coveralls, and sit at his counter for lunch. Other workers bought soft drinks and took them outside, where they would eat sandwiches from their lunch pails, while resting their backs against the wall of the diner.

"Don't forget to return those bottles," Mr. Goldberg would shout. "I didn't charge you for them."

Whenever I found a bottle on the sidewalk, I would take it inside. Papa laughed when I told him about the bottles. *"Ku-ichi-san,"* he would say, which was a sneaky way of saying "Jew" in Japanese. *Ku* is the Japanese word for nine and *ichi* means one, so together they make ten -- the Japanese word, *Ju.* Papa would explain: "Jewish no like hear Jew, like I no like hear Jap. Jewish smart with money," he would say, admiringly, "But stingy, even more stingy than Chinese."

But whenever Papa brought chickens home from Petaluma, he would give one to Mr. Goldberg. In return, Mr. Goldberg would invite us for breakfast the next day. "This one's on me, Mr. *Omi,*" he would say.

"No, no, I pay, Mr. Goldberg. You no make money if you give way."

Papa would order for all of us: Eggs fried sunny side up, ham, hash browns, toast, coffee for himself and Mama, and Ovaltine for *Shii-chan* and me. Mr. Goldberg's cooking was good, with just the right amount of salt; his potatoes were crunchy and moist; his bread was fresh baked from the oven. I loved to poke a fork into the yolk of my egg and watch it ooze onto the large oval plate so I could savor its taste with the hashbrowns. I would swab the puddles of yolk with my last piece of bread.

After coffee, Papa would try to pay, but Mr. Goldberg would never take his money. "Mr. *Omi,* I didn't pay you for the chickens, so you needn't pay me for breakfast. Friends don't pay each other money."

Papa once took a young Caucasian boy under his wing. He called him Brilliant-san, attaching the honorific, "san" to his last name, since his mother politely called Papa, Mr. *Omi* or *Omi-san.* Bob Brilliant had no father of his own, and his mother had been a customer for years. "Before you were born," Mama would say, "She was a good customer. She used to come in with her son, but not anymore. He's too grown up now." Mama liked them both.

Brilliant-san would listen avidly to Papa tell stories about Japanese soldiers, samurai valor and the might of the Japanese Navy. Papa told his stories in broken English from his pressing machine to anyone who would listen and walk to the counter if he thought the person was interested.

Brilliant-san was his best listener. He would often stop in on his way home from Galileo High School. He would set his books on the counter, and shout cheerfully, in a loud voice (even louder than Papa's), "*Omi-san, konnichi-wa, isogashii desuka?*" politely greeting Papa, and asking if he was busy. He had learned these phrases from Papa.

Papa would say (often irritated, at first, with Bob's brashness), "I busy Brilliant-san, but I take, maybe, five minutes for you."

And Bob would laugh and say, "Thank you, *Omi-san*. That is very kind of you."

Whenever Papa said a word that Bob didn't understand, Bob asked, "*Omi-san,* what did you just say?" Sometimes Papa would smile and say, "I no can say in English. If I say to you, I think you Mama mad at me."

During the summer, Bob would often come early. We couldn't see him from in back, but we knew it had to be him, because only he could stop the buzzing by unsticking the flapper on our front door. To stop the buzzing, Papa, who stood five feet tall in stocking feet, would have to stand on a chair to reach the flapper. At sixteen Bob was taller than six feet. When the buzzing stopped, it always had to be him.

"Hey, anybody home? Mr. *Omi*, are you there?" His voice resonated down the hallway. "It's me, Bob." He pounded on the counter bell. The sign next to the bell said, "Ring for Service."

"Why he ring bell when we already know he there?" Papa said.

Mama put her coffee down on the table and stood up.

"Let him wait," Papa said in Japanese.

Papa was in a foul mood. He'd been up till late, drinking the night before. *Rok-san* and I had been with him at the Nippon Bar. Papa frequently took me with him when he and *Rok-san* went out drinking. They had been celebrating the birth of *Komura-san*'s boy.

19

Komura-san had come to America with Papa on the same boat. After everyone, including *Komura-san,* had left, we were still at the bar.

"Just one more," Papa had said.

And for the third time, *Rok-san* told him, "We have to work tomorrow." Finally he was able to pull Papa away from the counter. Papa swayed, gripped *Rok-san's* shoulder, and smiled with red-veined eyes. Patting my head, he took one final gulp, and set the glass down. *Rok-san* looked at his watch, and said, "It's half past twelve."

This morning, Papa was paying the price with a hangover. With a checkered ice bag balanced on his head, he dropped an Alka-Seltzer tablet into a glass of water. Clearing his throat, he shouted in a raspy voice, "Oi, Brilliant-san, I eating now. You wait. I be out, OK?" He grimaced, took the ice bag off his head and gulped down the Alka-Seltzer

"Okay, Mr. *Omi*, I'll wait," Bob shouted back.

"Why did you leave the door unlocked?" Papa whispered a bit loudly to Mama in Japanese.

"Lots of ironing today. Mr. Green is picking up his suit before lunch time," she said, calmly.

Papa picked up *The Nichi-Bei Times* and held it up to the light. He placed the ice bag back on his head. Parting his lips, he sucked a loud s-s-s-s, then blew on his coffee. "Hakujins . . . why they so pushy?" he said. Despite his complaining, Papa liked Brilliant-san. He loved having a tall Caucasian, with hazel eyes, dark hair, and a long nose, as a mascot. "Like a stray dog," Papa would say to his friends, in Japanese, "that *Keto*, that hairy one, never stops returning," and he would laugh. But like Papa, Bob was not bashful. He would challenge Papa to an arm wrestling match at every opportunity.

Mama folded the newspaper and cleared the table. Papa continued to sip coffee noisily. "What could he possibly want so early in the morning?" he said, in Japanese. He set down the ice bag, finished his coffee, and left the table.

"Brilliant-san, why you here so early?" Papa said gruffly.

"*Ohayo gozai-masu*. Good morning. I want to show you my Charles Atlas training manual."

"Too early talk about maps," Papa snapped, rubbing his head.

"No, *Omi-san*, this is a book about building muscles."

"You read book get strong? Very good, Brilliant-san," Papa said, warming to Bob in spite of himself. "When you go see World's Fair on Treasure Island? You mama take you?"

"No, she's very busy. Maybe next week a friend and I will go."

"Tomorrow we go. You come?"

"I don't think so, Mr. *Omi*. I don't have any money."

"That's okay, I pay. You ask you mama okay you go."

"That's great! She's at work right now, but I'll ask her tonight and let you know first thing in the morning."

"We go ten o'clock sharp."

"No problem, *Omi-san*. I'll be on time. Oh, by the way, I think I can beat you now that I've read this Charles Atlas book." Bob placed his right arm on the counter across from Papa.

"You read and now you strong? Ha, ha, very good Brilliant-san." Papa rolled up the sleeve of his shirt and flexed his arm. His biceps looked like a Bull Durham sack packed with sand.

"How much you bet, Brilliant-san?"

"I'll bet you my allowance, one dollar, okay?"

"Okay but be sure use all you power."

Bob had a long forearm; when he flexed his arm, a bump about the size of a penny gumball lumped at his biceps.

Papa counted, "*Ichi, ni, san!*"

Hands locked together, arms quivering, each tried to pull the other's arm down, until finally, Papa's hand bent Bob's hand back, and slammed his arm down on the counter. Breathing hard, Papa said, "You getting more power than before -- maybe book help you -- five more years maybe you surprise -- maybe you beat me." He laughed, then added, "You owe me allowance, but I no need. You save for books, okay?"

Bob grinned. "Thanks *Omi-san*, but one of these days I'll beat you. I'm sure it won't take five years, you'll see."

Papa laughed again. He couldn't help but like Brilliant-san.

Brilliant-san never tired of Papa's stories, especially ones about Japanese warships. Whenever Papa told him that a Japanese ship was due to arrive in San Francisco, Bob got as excited as Papa. He'd set his books down on the counter and study the picture of the warship in Papa's newspaper.

"Wow, a battleship, *Omi-san*? Can I go with you?"

Papa always knew days in advance of a ship's arrival by reading about it in *The Nichi Bei Times*. He would go into the storeroom and emerge with a box full of Japanese books. After a quick search, he would say triumphantly, "Here it is! I found it!"

He would put it on the table and thumb through it. When he found the warship, he would read its statistics aloud: weight, size, equipment, capacity and whatever else caught his fancy.

Papa would drive us to the pier in his Studebaker sedan. Bob would sit in front with his back bent over and say, "I don't know why they don't build these cars bigger, *Omi-san*."

Papa would shake his head and say, "You getting too big," and point to the lever under the seat. "Push back seat, Brilliant-san."

At the pier, we would watch in awe as the gray behemoth slipped quietly into its berth. *Shii-chan* would hold Papa's hand, while I stood next to Bob. Uniformed sailors would moor the ship to the pier. A white flag with a red circle would flutter from its stem. Above the high-water line, in English, black letters as tall as three men standing head to foot would be the ship's name. Spectators, mostly Japanese, would point at the ship and say, "*Gunkan . . .*" Bob loved the word. He'd point at the ship and say to me, "*Gunkan, gunkan, gunkan!*"

Papa would smile and nod proudly. "Japanese boat very beautiful, *ne* Brilliant-san? I come this country on Persia Maru. Only take three week. Japanese boat very fast. American boat no can keep up. Japanese navy number two in world. *Igirisu* -- England -- number one."

We climbed the gangplank and walked from bow to stem and then followed a Japanese sailor down metal steps to a dining room and sleeping quarters. Back up on deck, we looked at the cannons, lifeboats, and rigging.

When we returned to the pier, Brilliant-san said to Papa, "That's one helluva ship, *Omi-san.*"

Papa beamed. He liked hearing that from a *Hakujin*. For days after boarding the ship, I walked around the cleaners saying, "*Gunkan, gunkan, gunkan,*" as proudly as Papa.

Chapter Six

More than two thousand Americans had died at Pearl Harbor. And in an instant, Papa's dreams had vanished. Suddenly, he had become more than an unwanted guest; he was an enemy of the nation. Would there be reprisals? Were we, the only Japanese in this neighborhood, safe? Where could we go?

In the days that followed the bombing, the FBI had quickly arrested many of the leading men in the Japanese community without warning. Their wives had no idea of where their husbands were taken, and men like Papa and *Rok-san* thought they would be next. But for many Japanese, this feeling was mixed with hopeful anxiety. Japan could win this war, they thought. Even a few Americans feared an invasion of California.

When Mr. Goldberg learned that the FBI were arresting Japanese in San Francisco, he came across the city to see us. We hadn't seen him since leaving Polk Street.

"U-w-a-h, Mr. Goldberg, you looking very healthy," Papa said. "How's business? You still on Polk Street?"

"Yes, Mr. *Omi*, and I'm doing just fine." He removed his hat. "I heard about the arrests."

"I scare," Papa said. "I no do nothing wrong." He beckoned toward the living quarters in back. "You like something to drink?"

"No, Mr. *Omi*, thank you just the same. I just wanted to see how you and your family were."

"You come inside anyway. I close door so customer no can come in."

"Oh no, *Omi-san*, you don't have to do that on my account."

"Business rotten. No make difference, door open or close."

Once inside our kitchen, Mr. Goldberg said, "Why should you be afraid? You and your wife have lived here longer than I have. And your children. I remember when they were born. You are not a citizen because the United States government has not let you and your friends become citizens. I've always thought that was unfair."

"Government no like Japanese," Papa said. "That's why Japan bomb Hawaii. Maybe even California not safe."

"Do you think they will invade California?" Mr. Goldberg asked.

"I think, maybe, if they think they have good chance . . ." Papa said.

"It's a long way from Japan," said Mr. Goldberg. "I think if they wanted to, they would have come by way of Hawaii. But now that we are ready for them, they may not."

"Maybe you right," Mr. Goldberg, "Papa said. "But I no think Japan bomb Hawaii. That big surprise. Everyone surprise. I know no what Japan do next."

"In any event, Mr. *Omi*, I'm glad you and your family are all right. If you need me for any reason, please call me. You have my phone number, do you not?"

"Yes. Thank you very much Mr. Goldberg." Papa gripped his hand and shook it vigorously. "I appreciate very much . . ."

After the initial flurry there were no more arrests. Still, Papa and his friends wondered, what would they do next? Then, the army posted signs all over the city. Military areas like the Presidio were off-limits to enemy aliens and persons of Japanese ancestry. Despite these notices Papa seemed relaxed. At least his telephone conversations seemed less frantic, though he still called *Rok-san* every night. Oddly, I felt as though we were trapped. We stayed away from places like Fisherman's Wharf, the Embarcadero and Hunters Point. Papa was afraid of being arrested.

Nevertheless, by the end of December Papa was speaking jovially to his customers once more. Always the consummate businessman, he bought US Savings stamps for the war effort and gave them away in return for business. He also helped the Civil Defense Officer during blackout drills, when the sound of high pitched sirens rang in our ears and beams of light moved across the sky. He would turn off the lights in our store, put on a white helmet, and walk down the street. He would rap on doors and store windows with his flashlight, and ask the occupants to turn off their lights. But when he got back, he would turn his Gilfillan radio on and shout with glee when the announcer described another Japanese victory in the Pacific.

At first, customers fearful of an invasion, asked Papa if he would help them if we were attacked. "Of course," he would say each time, "I born in Hiroshima and my family live in Yokohama. I give them Johnny Walker, Black Label, then they no hurt me. If I say you my friend, they no hurt you."

"Thank you, Mr. *Omi*. I feel much better now."

Papa would laugh graciously; it was unusual to see him so magnanimous. But nothing came of the threat of an invasion, except for a report of a Japanese submarine off the coast of Santa Barbara and one near Seattle. No shots were fired. But, of course, if shots had been fired, I don't know what Papa would have done. I'm sure he wouldn't have taken sides with Japanese soldiers against the *Hakujins*, though he liked to think that he would.

Chapter Seven

Before the war, Papa had Hollywood vanities. He loved the movies. His favorite stars were Bogart and Cagney; we went to see them often at the Alhambra or Royal Theaters on Polk Street. Papa told friends that he liked Janet Gaynor and Alice Faye too, even though there were rumors that one of them had said a Japanese man touched her improperly in a crowd. Papa laughed at the rumor. "She very good acting, but I no think Japanese man touching her. Maybe she just say, so everybody think she very good for touching," Papa told a salesman.

When Papa wore his vested pinstripe suit and trimmed his mustache like Dick Powell, he was at his Hollywood best. He would adjust his gray felt hat just so. "This: Stetson," he would say, smiling at his reflection in the mirror, "Six and five eighths."

Papa loved to drink and tell stories during dinner. He presided like a king over our household, squatting in boxer shorts on a cushion on the seat of a wooden chair instead of letting his feet touch the cold kitchen floor. We couldn't leave the table before he did. He loved to tell about the samurai warriors he had enacted on the stage.

"*Musashi*, he *ronin*. A masterless samurai. Very good with sword: in one motion, he cut same time he wipe off blood on sleeve and put blade into scabbard. When he walk away, his enemy look like he drunk. How you say?"

"Stagger . .?" I volunteered.

"Yes," Papa smiled drunkenly, pleased with the word. "He stagger. Big cut on head. He bleeding. Still he no can find handle. Then he fall down . . . die. Like this. See, I show you." Getting off his chair, he mimed stumbling, caught himself, and moved to a space between the kitchen and the dining room. Turning his head, he looked over his shoulder surreptitiously. He saw his imaginary adversary and smiled. Standing in a wide stance, he dropped his hand to the handle of his imaginary sword. Then, leading with his shoulder, he took a single step forward. Both hands moved quickly, cutting his opponent and returning his blade to its scabbard in one smooth motion.

With an exuberant laugh, he walked away. In that moment, he WAS Musashi. He had played this part with his younger brother, *Rok-san*, at *Kinmon* Hall on the corner of Bush and Buchanan Street in Japanese Town. "You know," he would say, "Takes practice put blade into scabbard with no looking. When blade go in. It fit tight. If miss even little bit, cut finger." Papa would laugh, and Mama, Shii-chan, and I would laugh with him, even though we'd heard this story more than once. We couldn't help it; Papa was a good actor.

But Papa had curious habits too. Before a bath (he took one almost every night), he would lay newspapers on the linoleum, squat in his underwear, and brush his head with two small brushes. Dandruff and hair would drift down onto the newspaper. When he was through, he would pick up the edges of the paper and shake everything into the center. Then he would fold it into smaller and smaller squares, making certain that nothing spilled before tossing it into a waste paper basket. Afterward he would shine his shoes while the water for his bath was running. When the tub was full, he would hurry into the bathroom and close the door.

Much later, he would come out all shiny and clean and tell Shii-chan and me, "Use my water; it clean, Japanese always clean no matter rich or poor. We take bath every day. Not like *Hakujin*."

Shii-chan and I would climb reluctantly into Papa's bath water after Mama had drained it by a third and run in more hot water. But when the two of us had finished bathing, the water looked like curdled cream. Not clear like Papa's. I was ashamed of how dirty we were.

One night I peeked through a crack in the door and was astonished to see Papa step out of the tub, drain it, and then carefully clean and refill it. No wonder his water was so clean! Now I knew, but instead of feeling better about how dirty *Shii-chan* and I were, I was sorry I had watched. Now Papa seemed more like us, and somehow I was disappointed.

While Mama bathed us, she would tell us stories about her life in Japan before she came to America and how she finally got here. "I grew up with my brother," she told us one time in her quiet, high-pitched voice. "I was five years old when my mother left for America. I lived with my father's step grandmother and grandfather."

"Your mother LEFT you when you were five?" *Shii-chan* asked, eyes wide.

"Yes, because my father was already in America. He went after the Japanese-Russian war because American companies advertised for laborers at three to four times the wages in Japan. They planned to send for us as soon as they had saved enough money."

Mama said that her father's parents had a large house with a yard full of trees, where her brother, uncle *Yoshio*, and she would play. "He was two years older and because he was a boy, my grandparents treated him much better," she said.

"So I was afraid to ask for things. My step-grandmother scolded me once because my sandals were dirty and worn. She complained about how expensive my new sandals were even though she bought me the cheapest pair in the store. She was always asking my grandfather about the money my parents sent from America. My grandfather was hardly ever home. He liked to drink with his friends."

Like Papa, I thought, but I didn't say anything. Instead I said, "Your grandmother was mean."

"So was her grandfather," *Shii-chan* said.

"Anyway," Mama continued, "When my parents finally sent for us, *Yoshio* didn't want to go. 'Who wants to live with smelly, hairy barbarians?' he said. "So my father hired a woman to look after me on the boat. I had so much fun. I could run upstairs, downstairs, go anywhere I wanted to."

"Wow," I said. It sounded like fun, but I couldn't imagine Mama running up and down stairs like a child.

"When we docked in San Francisco, I felt strange. I didn't know what to call my father. I was only eight months old when he left."

"You didn't even know what he looked like?" I asked.

"Sort of, but when he called out my name at the pier, I was too shy to call him *Otoo-san*."

"What did you call him if you couldn't call him Father?" *Shii-chan* asked. By now the water was getting cold, but we were too interested in Mama's story to care.

"I didn't call him anything. I just smiled and waved to him from the boat. I was so proud because my father was tall and handsome. A few of the women on board had treated me rudely because I was young, but when they saw my father, they suddenly became very friendly." She laughed.

"But the immigration officials wouldn't let me leave until I passed the physical examination at Angel Island. It took several days, so my father had to go back to Stockton and come back for me when I was through. After he came back from Stockton, he took me to a store and bought me American clothes."

"What did he buy you?" *Shii-chan* asked

"Dresses, silk stockings, shoes, skirts, blouses, everything, even a hat with a wide brim. He asked the lady who worked in the store to pick out what I needed."

Mama soaped my back with a towel and her eyes were watery. "But when we got to Stockton, my mother was very angry at me. She told me, 'We are very busy this time of year and because of you your father has had to make two trips to San Francisco.'"

"But that wasn't your f-a-u-l-t . . ." *Shii-chan* said, dragging out the word.

"Wasn't she even happy to see you?" I asked.

Mama shook her head. "I came during the busiest time of year; the hotel was full of guests."

"What did Grandpa say?" I asked.

"He wasn't there. A few days later, my mother scolded me again for something I said. 'Don't tell people you came in steerage,' she told me, 'Tell them you came first class.'"

"Why would she want you to say that?" *Shii-chan* asked.

"She probably didn't want people to think she was a penny pincher," I said.

Poor Mama, I thought. Not seeing her mother for more than eight years, hoping to be embraced, only to be scolded.

But my grandmother's life had changed during the years that Mama was in Japan. She cooked and cleaned all day with a five-year-old son tugging at her apron. With Mama, she had someone to help her.

When they went to the store, though, Mama felt unloved when her mother told her, "You are too old for ice cream. Ice cream is for children." While her younger brother ate his ice cream, Mama wiped his face. Always, she wiped his face; no one wiped hers.

Mama was born in Japan, but she was less Japanese than Papa. She finished high school in Stockton and went to business school to learn typing and shorthand. She spoke English like a *Nisei* since she had helped raise her *Nisei* brother. Unlike Papa, who sprinkled English words into Japanese sentences, Mama did the opposite.

I never once saw them hold hands. Papa always walked briskly ahead and Mama followed behind him, as Japanese women do in Japan. But to his consternation, she didn't display the manners and affectations of a typical Japanese woman. "Why can't you behave more graciously?" he would ask her in Japanese. I knew what he meant. *Obasan*, my aunt, knew the proper etiquettes. She fussed over and flattered *Rok-san's* friends with small compliments, fluttering in and out of the kitchen with trays of food and drink.

Poor Mama. She withstood Papa's criticisms silently, only slamming pots and pans in the kitchen when he spoke unkindly about her brothers. One evening after he'd had a few drinks, I heard him teasing her in the kitchen. With a thick-tongue, he told her, "Your brother is a good-for-nothing laggard. If it weren't for your father, he'd have nothing. He can't even speak Japanese properly," then laughed.

Mama screamed and told him to stop. Pulling pots and pans out of the cupboard, she began throwing them around the kitchen. I lay in bed frightened at what might happen next. But Papa didn't strike Mama. He just shouted obscenities at her, slammed the kitchen door, and went into the bathroom. When he climbed into bed, I pretended to be asleep; I only rolled over after I heard him snore and heard Mama's slippered feet shuffle past my bed.

Mama's slippers shuffled everywhere. Slap, slap, slap down the hallway to my bed or into the kitchen. I heard them often, especially when I was sick. Measles, mumps, scarlet fever, pneumonia -- I caught them all. But pneumonia worried Mama most. She blamed Papa for my poor health, since he often kept me out late. The doctor told them I could die if I had pneumonia again.

On cold nights, Mama wrapped *yutampos* -- one-gallon bottles, usually empty shoyu bottles filled with hot water -- in bath towels

31

and placed them under the covers near my feet. She placed a battered kettle on a kerosene stove near my head, which whistled and steamed all night, s-i-i-i-i-i . . . But in the mornings, the *yutampos* were a delight. The unwrapped bottles were warm to the touch. I'd wrap my arms around them and press the smooth, warm glass to my cheek.

I was six or seven the first time I had pneumonia. I'd never felt so miserable in my life. "Leave me alone," I whined to Mama. But she wouldn't listen. She made me drink water until it dribbled out of my mouth. "This will help break the fever," she insisted, using a towel to catch the excess water. While I lay there wondering what she would do next, she went into the kitchen. I could hear a tapping against a pan, and knew what she was up to. She was pouring Coleman's mustard out of a small can into a pan of water. She poked and stirred at the concoction with a chopstick, breaking down the lumps of mustard. I could see the yellow powder becoming paste. I pictured her spreading the paste on a cheesecloth, covering it with another layer of cloth, spreading more paste, then another layer of cloth, paste, cloth, paste, until she had a thick blanket of mustard. Shuffling into my room, slap, slap, she unbuttoned my shirt and placed this hot blanket gently on my chest.

"U-u-u, oh-ooo," I protested, holding my breath. I took short breaths through my nose, trying not to breath in the fumes, but the smell was inescapable. I lay very still so the mustard wouldn't spill out onto the bedclothes.

I could hear Papa in the hallway after closing the store. Turning the light on over my head, he told Mama to move away in Japanese. He shook a thermometer vigorously, and held it to the light. As I lay there with the skinny end of the thermometer under my tongue, he whispered, "Lay still."

I didn't dare move. He timed one minute with his watch, and then said, "Okay." I felt the etched lines slide across my lips when the thermometer slid out. I sighed with relief, while he held the thermometer up to the light. But after reading the numbers, he shook his head, turned off the light, and went into the kitchen.

During the night, after several more readings, Mama removed the mustard plaster and replaced it with a hot one. Again, I held my breath and lay still. I wanted to crawl out of bed, go into the kitchen, and empty the mustard can into the sink, but I was too weak. And then I prayed, hoped that by some miracle, my fever would go down. But, no. Slap, slap, slap. Mama was in the hallway. I held my breath and heard Papa snoring on the sofa. Slap, slap, slap into the kitchen. Mama's slippers kept me up all night, until I awoke in the morning and my fever was broken.

Once in a while, Papa and Mama would have a good laugh together, usually when I did something foolish, like the time I wore Papa's shoes to school and embarrassed him in front of my teacher. I didn't understand their need to show everyone that we were as well off as most everyone else. We weren't paupers, but we weren't rich either. It was during a time when most everything I wore -- jackets, shirts and trousers -- could be bought inexpensively at Penney's, or else Mama could alter a garment to fit me off the unclaimed garment rack.

But shoes weren't dry-cleaned. We didn't have racks of unclaimed shoes, so Papa had to take me to the store to buy them. By the time I was eight or nine, trips to the shoe store became more frequent, often within three to four months of our last visit. And Papa would tease me. He would say that he had shoes in his closet that were older than me, but still like new. And I took him to mean that I was wearing them out faster than he could afford to buy them. So when my Buster Brown's with the metal toe plates had worn through and were beyond cardboard repair (Mama would fashion soles out of cardboard and place them inside my shoes), I came up with an idea: Papa's shoes. He had a pair with crepe soles in the closet that weren't shiny (the soles along the edges looked like old bubblegum), but had some mileage left. I'd worn them around the cleaners on rainy days to play in, and I didn't think Papa would mind my wearing them to school – in fact, I was sure my classmates would be envious.

But when I pulled them out of the closet and put them on, they suddenly felt loose and heavy. I was sure they'd be fine once I got outside, but they weren't. My feet kept slipping and sliding. I would set my lunch pail down and retie the laces; but no matter how tightly I tied them, after a few steps, I'd begin to feel my feet sliding again. When I finally made it to school, the yard was empty; second bell had already rung. I went quietly through the empty hallway, and I soon discovered that I could slide on the shiny floor. Instead of lifting my feet, I skated. But sometimes my sole would stick and I would stumble. I tried to skate into my classroom, but my sole stuck again and I stumbled through the door. Mrs. Prichard, my third grade teacher, peered at me over her glasses and said, sternly, "*Minoru*, you're tardy." She picked up a pencil and wrote something in her notebook.

During recess, while dodging a ball, I slipped the wrong way and twisted my ankle. It hurt so badly that the janitor had to carry me into the nurse's office. The nurse wrapped my ankle and asked if I knew my phone number.

When she phoned the cleaners, I could hear Papa's voice. It was so loud that the nurse had to hold the phone away from her ear.

A few minutes later, I heard Papa's voice again, but this time in the empty hallway. "Where is my son? Where is my son?" His voice echoed, then more voices followed by the click clacks of high-heeled shoes.

Papa, the principal, and Mrs. Prichard came into the nurse's room. "Here's your son, Mr. *Omi*," Mrs Prichard said, with a smile. "I think he'll be fine. He just twisted his ankle during recess. The nurse says you should take him home to rest."

"Thank you very much, "Papa said politely. "*Minoru* make big mistake this morning. He put on wrong shoes. Very sorry. Then he said to me in Japanese, "*Do-shite son-na ton-de-mo nai kutsu-o hai-ta no*. Why on earth did you wear those ungodly shoes?"

"Mine had big holes," I said, making a circle with a thumb and forefinger.

Papa's face turned red. "Thank you," he said to Mrs. Prichard again. Shaking her hand, then the principal's, then the nurse's, he lifted me off the bed and carried me out to the car. I worried all the way home, but when we got there, he laughed, and told Mama what happened.

"*Minoru* said that in front of everybody?" Mama said, her eyes wide. Then, they both laughed for a long time. That night we went to J. C. Penney's for a pair of high top sneakers.

Chapter Eight

I often felt comforted and secure to know that Papa and Rok-san remained together like a pair of comfortable sneakers. But unlike sneakers that followed one after the other, they took comfort in being together alone. They frequently felt homesick in a foreign land, thousands of miles away from home, having to adapt themselves to the way of Westerners. They often had a yearning to return home even though home was not a place with traditional virtues. Their father had no warm feelings for a fifth and sixth born son. They were expendable, without value in a Japanese family. This was hard to accept, even though, eventually, they overcame such feelings of despair.

When their father had left America to return to Japan, his authority through their eldest brother in America had been enormous. But, in time, his influence dwindled, until finally, they wrested themselves away. From then on, Papa and *Rok-san* were inseparable, and *Kazuo*, their eldest brother, became their antagonist. He came to represent the tyranny that once was their father.

Papa had been summoned to America in 1917, when he was just sixteen. Then came *Rok-san,* younger by three years, six months later. But even before them, *Kazuo,* their eldest brother, older than Papa by fifteen years, had sailed to America in 1901, and became the first of the *Omi* family to emigrate to America. After working odd jobs, *Kazuo* earned enough money to return to Japan for a bride in 1908, and return to America again.

By 1914, *Kazuo* had two sons. His wife was expecting a third child, a daughter, when he summoned his father from Japan to help build a chicken ranch in Petaluma. A year later Papa and *Rok-san* were summoned to America as well. After placing them in *Kazuo's* care, their father returned to Japan. And that is how *Kazuo* replaced their father as the tyrant of the family.

Kazuo sent money back to Japan regularly, but Papa and *Rok-san* felt deprived. They hadn't seen the money that was theirs, and they hadn't received any words of thanks from home. Privately, they rebelled, and took out their frustrations on *Kazuo*. They began to resent him, and finally, one day, Papa told *Kazuo*, "No more. We are not your children. We are adults and have our own lives to live. We have done enough for you and our family in Japan."

Living away from home for so long had changed their feelings. *Kazuo*, being the first-born son, had only assumed his father's role out of duty -- that was his fate. But no matter, Papa and *Rok-san* felt they had given more than their fair share. *Kazuo* had not given them good reason to do more.

Eventually, *Kazuo* had asked for money to build a family monument in a cemetery in Yokohama, and that was the last straw. "Why?" Papa had asked. "There is already a large family tomb in Hiroshima. It has been in our family for centuries."

"Father says it is too far," *Kazuo* said. "He wants one close to where they live. He says he will give you and *Rokuro* favorable recognition for helping to build it."

"All right," Papa said to *Kazuo*, "We will help only this once more, but tell father not to ask for any more money. We need money ourselves to survive in America."

This was in 1931, the year that *Rok-san* and Obasan lost their first child at birth, and a year after I was born. Shortly after that, they lost a girl. They wanted to have children like *Shii-chan* and me, but couldn't. The miscarriage of their second child had taken such a toll on *Obasan* that the doctor advised them against trying for anymore. And *Rok-san*, in a fit of pique, went out and bought a dog, a tan terrier with short hair. In short time, he and *Obasan* grew to love their dog. *Obasan* called her *Poochie*.

They soon discovered that *Poochie* was more human than dog. She quickly learned to sit, shake hands, bow, stand, speak, stay, and fetch. She even learned to pray, an unusual act for a dog, particularly since *Rok-san* and *Obasan* were not churchgoers.

"*Oinori-se*. Pray," *Rok-san* would say, and *Poochie* would sink to the floor, cross her front paws and lower her head.

"Good girl," *Rok-san* would say, stroking her back. He would give her a slice of *takuan* and chuckle.

"*Poochie* must be Japanese," he would say to Papa in Japanese, "How else can you explain the way she relishes Japanese pickles?"

And Papa would reply, "*S-o-h . . . Poochie wa fushigi ja. Poochie* is remarkable."

Whenever we went to see *Rok-san* and *Obasan*, *Poochie* would sit quietly while *Rok-san* scratched her back. And whenever he left the table to go to the icebox, she would follow him, wagging her tail. "How would you like something to whet your appetite?" *Rok-san* would ask her in Japanese, unscrewing the lid of a *takuan* jar. And an unmistakable odor would settle in to the kitchen.

"Pee yew," I would say, turning my head. *Rok-san* would chuckle and fish a radish pickle out of the jar.

"*Anata*," *Obasan* would giggle from the sink, "You mustn't use your fingers."

Rok-san would laugh, slice the pickled radish into bite-sized slices, and offer a slice to *Poochie*. When she would only sniff at it and open her mouth to take it from *Rok-san's* hand, *Rok-san* would ask her in Japanese, "Have you forgotten, *Poochie*?" And she would remember. Sinking to the floor, she would cross her paws and lower her head.

"Good girl," *Rok-san* would say, stroking her head. Then, he would place the food near her snout and let her take it gently between her teeth.

Poochie was sensitive as well. She understood *Rok-san's* voice inflections. If *Rok-san* would say quietly, "Get in the box," she would know it was time to bed down. Fetching her blanket, she would crawl into her crate. But if *Rok-san* teased her, telling her in a harsh voice, "*Poochie*, fetch your blanket and get in your box," she knew he was only teasing. Growling softly, she would wag her tail and wait to hear his reassuring voice.

Rok-san was my favorite uncle, but he was always more friend than uncle. Sometimes I would call him "*Ojisan*," the proper word for uncle, as the word, "*Obasan*," was proper for aunt. But more often than not, I called him by his nickname *Rok-san* like Papa and his friends did. He didn't seem to mind what I called him. He never raised an eyebrow. I thought I knew him well until I grew older; then I wasn't sure. But in my mind he would always be a generous and fun-loving man. Like Papa he loved to tell stories, but unlike Papa, *Rok-san* often made fun of himself.

"I was only twelve or thirteen when I came to America," he often told us, in Japanese. I was spoiled by my mother, because I was the youngest. But *Kazuo* didn't baby me. In fact, he had very little patience with me. He constantly scolded me to do this and that. Finally I had to leave him and the chickens to find other work in the city.

"My first job," he said, "Was in a Japanese laundry . . ." He said he had been working there for less than a month when he tried sneaking wind into the workplace. "We used to dip our irons into a cooling vat," he said, "And the noise was very loud that morning. Everyone was trying to make a good impression on *Noguchi-san*, the foreman. With all that sizzling, I didn't think anyone would hear it. They couldn't see me, either, the room was fogged over."

"But it sounded like air from a pinched balloon, *bi-ri, bi-ri*," he imitated, laughing, "Much louder than I expected. And the smell was so strong that even I had to wave a hand in front of my face. When the woman behind me gasped, I turned and whispered, 'Sorry . . . pork and beans.' The other ironers, who had been intent on their ironing with backs bent, stopped working and looked at each other accusingly. Then they began fanning their faces. *Noguchi-san* pinched his nose and left the room."

Rok-san chuckled as he remembered the looks on everyone's faces. "When I saw them looking at each other, I couldn't keep myself from laughing. But no one else thought it was funny. When they discovered it was me, everyone left the room."

"Later on, *Noguchi-san* warned me: 'Stoppages like that cost money,' he said. But something wonderful happened that day. For the first time, the workers in the ironing room talked to each other. And after that, whenever I walked into the room, they would fan their faces and laugh. I didn't care what *Noguchi-san* had said. Their friendliness made it all worthwhile."

Rok-san and Papa loved to tell each other stories about their friends. They joked about speech impediments, crooked mouths, smelly breath, body odors, and whatever else struck them as funny. *Rok-san* liked to mimic *Ishikawa-san*, a man who had a habit of coughing up and re-swallowing his food. "*Ni-do-gui-san*." or "Twice-eating man," Papa would say, overcome with laughter.

Rok-san would laugh too. "I wish you would tell him to stop doing that; how can he not know he has such a disgusting habit?"

Ishikawa-san usually came into our cleaners just as we were about to have dinner. Sniffing the air appreciatively, he would complement Mama on her cooking. Papa would laugh, hang the "closed" sign on the door, and invite him in back. At first, *Ishikawa-san* would refuse politely, shaking his head, no, while trying to unlock the shop door. But Papa would steer him into our living room.

Over dinner, they would joke and trade stories about Japan and how they had come to America on the same boat. Every so often *Ishikawa-san* would stop, cough, and then swallow. I would remember *Rok-san's* mimics and try hard not to laugh. Red-faced, Papa would tell me sternly to stop playing at the table. *Ishikawa-san* would look at me, not understanding, and then continue his story. After a while he would stop again and repeat his habit. Finally, I would have to leave the table and finish my dinner in the kitchen.

Papa and *Rok-san* would take turns imitating him. "No, no, no," *Rok-san* would say, "Like this, see . . . " He would move his jaws rapidly, while smacking his lips, then swallow quickly. His Adam's apple would bob up and then down. "*Ahhh* . . ." he would say, pausing a moment with his eyes closed. Then "*Ahhhh* . . . " again.

"Yes, yes . . ." Papa would say enthusiastically, "That was perfect!" Then they would laugh until their eyes watered.

Obasan, *Rok-san* 's wife, was a woman that other women envied with scorn, Mama included -- but Papa and his friends delighted in her. She had an oval face, a pale, smooth complexion, and thin eyebrows, mere silhouettes, over eyes that twinkled. Her lips were thin, smooth and shiny with lipstick. She spoke in a high-pitched, lyrical voice, and covered her mouth when she giggled.

Whenever Papa and I stopped at their cleaners, she would quietly put on her coat and go out the door. She would return loaded down with two brown bags, which she carried into the kitchen. A little later she would come into the work area and set a tray of drinks and snacks on a table near the pressing machine. While Papa and *Rok-san* traded stories, drank and snacked, *Obasan* would phone a Chinese restaurant.

Papa always looked surprised when the delivery man came to the door. "Oh, no . . . not again," he would say, "We were about to leave."

"No, no," she would tell him. "You have to stay. We can't return all this food." They would banter back and forth in this way, while she set the table in their living room.

"We stay," Papa would say, finally, "But I pay."

After an evening of eating, drinking, and talking, Papa would rise from the sofa, take out his wallet, and place several bills on the table. "What are you doing?" *Obasan* would say, sticking the money into my pocket. I would pull out the money and put it back on the table. She would stuff the bills back inside my pocket and usher me out the door. I would put them in her apron pocket and hurry to the car. She would follow me to the car, open the door, and throw the money on the seat. If the doors were locked, she would pin the bills under the windshield wiper, run back inside, and lock the door behind her.

"She crazy," Papa would laugh, while driving away.

On the Christmas morning of the year before Japan attacked Pearl Harbor, *Rok-san* and *Obasan* came to our cleaners with gifts. "Wow!" I said when I saw the bicycle.

"Do you like the color?" *Obasan* asked anxiously.

"You shouldn't have," Mama said.

"You do too much," Papa told them.

Rok-san chuckled, looking pleased.

It wasn't any ordinary bike; it was a shiny gray and white Schwinn, man-sized, with chrome trim, balloon white-wall tires, leather seat, horn, battery-operated headlight, kickstand, fenders, and coaster brakes. Did I mind the color? I loved it! I nearly cried. I had never dreamed of owning such a bicycle, and couldn't wait to ride it.

"*Shii-chan*," I heard *Obasan* say to *Shii-chan*, "We have something for you too."

She gave her a large box covered with shiny Christmas paper and tied with a big bow, but I didn't care what *Shii-chan* was getting; I wanted to take my bike outside. In pajamas and bare feet, I wheeled it out the door. The sidewalk felt cold, but I didn't mind. I walked the bike down to Broadway, where the street was level. Leaning the bike against a brick wall, I climbed on and balanced myself on the seat.

My feet barely reached the pedals, so I moved off the seat and straddled the bar. Pushing off from the wall, I began to pedal. Wobbling from building to curb and back again, I managed to stay on to the end of the block. After that, my bike and I were inseparable.

.Before the war, Papa and *Rok-san* drove us everywhere, on picnics to the Russian River, clam digging at Tomales Bay, and during the summer, to Santa Cruz. One weekend we even drove to Yosemite and back. On Sundays, we usually went to the Wander Inn, at a beach below Linda Mar. Early in the morning, after everything had been loaded into the car, Papa would go back into the cleaners and phone *Rok-san* while Mama, *Shii-chan*, and I waited in the car.

Finally, I'd have to go inside to get him. He would motion me away with a wave of his hand as if I were a pesky fly. Standing on the pedal of the pressing machine, I would wait impatiently. After a few minutes, I would nudge him again, and again he would wave me away. After a few more nudges, he would look at the clock on the wall and say in Japanese, "Let's talk about this later; they're waiting in the car. Adjusting the brim of his hat in the mirror, he would finally say, "We go now."

The drive to *Rok-san*'s cleaners was a circuitous route -- down Van Ness to Market, up to Twin Peaks, past St Francis Woods, and down Junipero Serra to Ocean Avenue. *Rok-san* and *Obasan* would be waiting outside their panel truck with *Poochie*. We would drive along Highway One past Pacifica, Sharp Park, and Rock-a-way Beach while *Rok-san* followed us. Once we reached the Wander Inn, we would have to wait again while Papa and *Rok-san* went inside to pay. The only way to the beach was through their gate and down a dirt road to a gravel lot.

Papa and *Rok-san* would often come running out of the tavern, one chasing the other, each shouting in Japanese that it was his turn to pay. One or the other would jump in his truck, roll up the window, and lock the door. When Papa did this to *Rok-san*, he would smile while starting the engine. But whenever *Rok-san* did this to Papa, Papa would return to our car, shaking his head in disbelief. Meanwhile, the tavern owner would come out and wait. He unsnapped the lock, and lowered the chain while Papa and *Rok-san* ran back and forth in the parking lot. Smoking a cigar, he would look disdainfully at us while we drove through the gate. When we left, the same man came out of the tavern and lowered the chain again.

From the parking lot to the beach, through shifting sand and clumps of ice plant, we carried armloads of umbrellas, blankets, fishing poles, the bait box, and grocery bags filled with food and drinks. We had to make two trips back and forth because Mama and *Obasan* loved to cook.

Mama and *Obasan* were so modest that they didn't wear bathing suits to the beach – though Papa, *Rok-san*, *Shii-chan* and I all wore them under our clothes. As soon as the windbreaks were in place, we took off our clothes and raced to the water. *Shii-chan*, *Poochie*, and I would watch Papa and *Rok-san* disappear into the breakers. After they returned from their swim, Mama and *Obasan* would serve *maki sushi*, *nishime*, *kamaboko*, *gobo*, potato chips and Belfast cola from the large economy size bottles. Even if Mama privately objected to *Obasan's* pretentious manners, she did not let on. We all had a good time at the beach. We often stayed to watch the sunset and sometimes kept warm by the fire until it got dark.

Chapter Nine

When Papa sold the cleaners in January of the year of the War, I was incredulous. "Why?" I asked. It was our home, where *Shii-chan* and I were born. I didn't want to move to our new cleaners in the Sunset. It was near the ocean, on the other side of the city. "You like when you see," Papa had said. *Never,* I thought. But we moved anyway. Had he known then, what the Prime Minister in Japan had been planning, we might have stayed.

Papa had long been unhappy with New City Cleaners. And my second eldest cousin George, had asked him to sell the cleaners to him and his younger brother, Ben. At first, Papa wasn't sure his nephews could run the business. After all, their father *Kazuo* hadn't been able to manage the ranch in Petaluma. "But that wasn't his fault," George pleaded. "Papa was swindled by that Stanford student."

Finally, Papa relented. He had wanted the other store badly.

Papa didn't like being outdone by *Rok-san* -- though he would never admit to it.. *Rok-san* and *Obasan* owned the Du-Rite Cleaners on Monterey Boulevard in San Francisco, and had recently bought new equipment and were planning to hire help.

Papa was envious. "How could *Rokuro* be so successful?" he asked Mama. "He was so frail when he came to America. He couldn't work. *Kazuo* kept scolding him."

"But that was more than twenty years ago," Mama said, "He was only twelve then."

Papa had tried to promote more business at New City Cleaners, but the man he hired turned out to be a cheat. Papa had given him commissions for garments to be cleaned and pressed from fictitious customers. When the garments hung unclaimed for months, Papa realized what had happened. But by then the swindler was gone.

Papa thought that *Rok-san's* success was due to the fact that his cleaners was much better located than ours. He explained that New City Cleaners was in an older neighborhood with stores and apartment buildings. "It's better to be around homes," he said in Japanese. "The new homes in the Sunset District should bring in more customers."

Papa and Mama taught my cousins George and Ben to press, iron and sew, to make sure they'd be ready to take over. More importantly, Papa showed them how to organize their work: from emptying pockets and removing buttons to tagging garments and checking them again before bundling them for the cleaning plant. "If you don't empty pockets, valuables will be lost at the cleaning plant, and if you don't take the buttons off, they will melt in the cleaning solution," Papa said. "Be sure and tag everything, if you don't, when the clothes come back from the plant, you won't know who they belong to.

"After you've pressed and ironed them, be sure to hang them in order with the most recent ones hanging near the front of the store, otherwise, when the customer comes to pick up his clothes you will have to look everywhere."

Papa also taught them to read the steam gauge and adjust the steam for the pressing machine boiler. He showed them how to fix the boiler if it leaked. He also gave them his list of customers for his delivery route.

Mama told me that when my cousins' mother died, my uncle wasn't ready to raise three children and manage a business at the same time. "He did the best he could," Mama said, "And we loaned him money . . . your cousins were unhappy. They came to our cleaners often and I fed them. Sometimes they slept over and stayed for weeks at a time. Your father remembered how well your cousin's mother treated him when he first came to America. That's why your father wanted to help them."

"But your uncle had to work hard. He was cheated just before your aunt died. A young Nisei had embezzled money from their joint bank account. You see, your uncle trusted this young man because he let him use his name on the deed. Japanese couldn't own land in California unless they were citizens."

"In the end, your uncle couldn't compete. The large companies took over the poultry business with machines. Your poor uncle was doing everything by hand. He had to sell everything. But then he bought a small store near Japanese town. But his children weren't interested in the grocery business, and your father and *Rok-san* were not much older than they were. Your cousins wanted to do what their uncles did."

After several trips to the Sunset District, and talking to agents, Papa found a store he liked. "This will be our new place," he told Mama, *Shii-chan* and me, while we sat in his new car. (He had surprised us the night before with a brand new Dodge sedan).

When we stepped out of the car, the wind blew in our faces. Mama shaded her face with one hand and held down her dress with the other. Papa held onto the brim of his hat. The air smelled like the beach, and the squares in the sidewalk were dusted with sand. The ocean was straight down Lawton Street, about a mile away. And five blocks around the corner, down 25th Avenue, was Golden Gate Park. I looked beyond our block and saw new homes under construction, but also saw empty blocks, girdled with sidewalks, containing mountains of sand.

When we looked inside the store, carpenters were hammering and sawing. "*Oi, Omi-san*" a man said, through the dust, in Japanese, "Does this counter location look okay to you'?"

"*Soh..*," Papa replied. "Where press machine going?"

"Over here." The workman pointed to a chalked circle on the cement floor.

Papa walked to where he thought the counter should be and motioned with his arms. "Then counter should be here, away from wall," he told him.

Pulling a stick of chalk out of his pocket, the workman marked the floor where Papa stood. We could see the beginnings of partitions, wood frames bolted to the floor, and cardboard boxes filled with broken pieces of plaster, splintered wood, and sawdust.

"How you like?" Papa asked

"I don't know," I said. "Okay, I guess."

We walked down the block past a cabinet store, a bar, a liquor store, a fabric store, and a barbershop. The corner lot was vacant. Across the street, more stores: a Safeway, a furniture store, a stationary store and a Walgreen's. Unlike Polk Street, which brimmed with activity, Lawton Street was deserted. "This Sunset District," Papa said proudly, as he drove us past homes and up to the reservoir on Moraga Street.

"This where we get water," Papa said, as though this reservoir was somehow important to our new quarters.

In the new shop, called Safety Cleaners, *Shii-chan* and I would sleep in a bunk bed against the wall of a small room with a partition. At first, it felt strange. Papa and I had always slept together for as long as I could remember. Stranger still, *Shii-chan* slept above me. Sometimes she would climb down the ladder and walk in her sleep. I didn't know she was sleep-walking, until one night, I stopped her once when we were both headed for the bathroom. I let her go first, but in the morning, she couldn't even remember that I had spoken to her. After that, I often wondered how long she'd been sleep-walking for.

"We do good here," Papa said about our new cleaners, "More better than before," he said as he pointed to the homes under construction. But these homes quickly became a problem for me. Everyone I met in school seemed to live in one except me. Suddenly to live in a house had meanings and feelings I couldn't describe. I felt ashamed. I couldn't invite friends into our makeshift quarters. Papa said it was because it was *mucha kucha*, or messy. Was he ashamed, too?

Whenever I played in the playground near our cleaners, everyone seemed friendly while we played, but after it closed, we went home in different directions. Whenever I walked by a house and saw lights in the window, I wondered how it felt to live inside one of them.

Shii-chan and I would walk five blocks to school. And I hadn't minded her walking with me, if she would only listen. Sometimes, I'd pretend to get mad to get her attention.

"Button up your coat and hurry up," I said, harshly.

"Why do I have to?" she said.

"I want to get home for the ball game."

"Why are you so bossy?" she persisted.

"Do as I say, it's getting cold."

"Hurry up," I said. The sun hid behind the clouds.

"I'm going as fast as I can."

I hated this street and wished we were on Polk Street. Nothing of interest around here except homes. Homes for *Hakujins*. We walked past the empty playground. Except for the sound of the bouncing ball, it was quiet. The ball made a panging sound. *Pang, pang, pang,* quiet, and then a thud, when it hit the backboard. Then *pang, pang, pang* again.

A boy in a green baseball cap looked toward us. He picked up the ball and walked to the fence. Cupping his hand to his mouth, he hollered, "Ching, chong Chinaman sitting on a fence. Hey, come over here Chinaman and sit on this fence." He laughed.

"Don't pay any attention," I said, "Just keep walking."

"We're not even Chinese," *Shii-chan* whispered.

"It doesn't matter," I said.

"Hey you chinks, come over here," the boy yelled again.

"Go bother someone else," I yelled back.

"What did he say?" the boy asked. Nodding his head, he handed the ball to another boy, went to the gate, flung it open and ran toward us. The two other boys followed him.

Without stopping to look, the boy cut across the street and slid across the sidewalk to where we stood.

Pressing his face close to mine, he glared. "What did you call me?" His face glistened with sweat; I could see his freckles and his pale, nearly invisible orange eyebrows. I took *Shii-chan's* hand and led her to an alcove.

"Hey wait a minute," he yelled. "Where d'you think you're going; come back here."

Walking back slowly, I told him, "I didn't call you anything. I only said to bother someone else."

"Listen, no Chinaman tells me what to do."

"I didn't tell you anything. I only asked. And I'm not a China-man."

"Oh yeah? What are you then? A monkey or something?" He pressed up to my chest.

"Neither," I said, "Will you keep away from me? We didn't do anything to you." And then I mumbled, "I'm sorry for what I said."

"Mick," a boy in a gray sweatshirt said, "Leave him alone. He said he's sorry." He pulled the red-haired boy away from me. "Come on, let's go shoot baskets."

"Aw, all right," the boy named Mick said, snatching the basketball away from the boy in the gray sweatshirt. The three boys crossed the street laughing, bouncing the ball back and forth.

I felt ashamed, but I was glad it was over. When I went to the alcove for *Shii-chan*, the sun felt warm on my back. I held out my hand to her, and she said, "We'd better hurry, Minoru, or else you'll miss the game."

Chapter Ten

Obasan was pregnant again, and she was overjoyed. "This time, I will be very careful," she said. "I will do exactly what the doctor says." As she grew large with the child, *Rok-san* would tease *Poochie*. "What are we going to do with you after the baby is born?" he would ask her, holding up a morsel of her favorite pickled radish.

Poochie would wag her tail and circle around him.

"*Poochie* will have a baby brother," *Obasan* would say, and *Rok-san* would laugh. He'd wait for *Poochie* to "pray," and then let her take the *takuan* from his hand.

Toward the end of November, a month before the attack on Pearl Harbor, I heard Papa say that Japanese diplomats had been kept waiting in front of the Senate Building in Washington, D. C. He'd seen it on a newsreel. It was another example of how poorly the Japanese were being treated by the Americans. "They no like Japanese," Papa said to a cleaning supply salesman.

"You're mistaken, Mr. *Omi*," the salesman said, closing the cover of his catalogue. "Japan is an ally."

"I no think so, Mr. Richie. America helping China."

"You shouldn't believe everything you hear, *Omi-san*. We're in no position to destroy our friendship with your country. Haven't you heard what's going on in Europe?"

"Hitler," Papa said disgustedly. "He same like Kaiser. I no like him. He making big trouble when I come to America in 1916."

"That's right, *Omi-san*. So you see, there's no need to worry. The problem is in Europe. Japan and America are allies."

The treatment of the envoy in Washington was quickly forgotten when *Rok-san*, a happy father, came into our cleaners with a box of blue-banded cigars. "What did you name him?" Papa asked, accepting several cigars.

"*Takashi*, after his grandfather."

"How is *Asaye*?" Mama asked in her high voice.

"She's fine, " *Rok-san* said. "The doctor said they should be home by this weekend."

"Can I come over and help?" Mama said.

"No. . . You know how she is. If you came over, she'd worry more about you than the baby."

Mama nodded; Papa laughed and blew smoke in the air. Everyone seemed happy. Christmas was not far off and I wondered what sort of presents *Shii-chan* and I would get this year.

But two weeks later, Japan attacked Pearl Harbor and whatever comfort we enjoyed was lost. Suddenly our lives were turned topsy-turvy. My birthday was only eight days away. And although birthday celebrations were never big in our family, I didn't get any presents that year, nor, for that matter did *Shii-chan* and I receive any Christmas presents from *Rok-san* and *Obasan*.

But Papa did buy a small Douglas fir, and he decorated it with lights that blinked on and off. He placed it at the end of the counter for customers to see. It was his way of saying, "See, we celebrate Christmas just like you."

Mama baked a turkey and pumpkin pie, and bought me a baseball glove and *Shii-chan* a dress for Christmas. Though we all took baths to be clean on New Year's Day, we did not celebrate it with a traditional Japanese feast.

Papa spoke to his friends daily. Only a few days after the bombing, important men in the Japanese community had been arrested: the minister of the Buddhist Church, the editor of the Japanese newspaper, Japanese school teachers, and the leaders of the Hiroshima *Kenjinkai* (a prefectural organization). They'd been whisked away without notice.

"The FBI didn't tell their wives anything," Papa said into the phone in Japanese. "No one knows where they are . . ."

But after the initial arrests, nothing else happened. Nonetheless, Papa and his friends were worried. "The government is afraid that we might do something bad," Papa told *Rok-san* on the phone. "*Sato-*

san, the barber, said that we have to get rid of anything that might look suspicious, anything Japanese."

After that, Papa and Mama looked into closets and drawers and pulled out dolls, scrolls, vases, knives, and lacquered boxes and anything made in Japan. Papa wrapped them in newspapers, and placed them in cardboard boxes.

Mama had always loved her dolls. She brought them out every year on Girls Day, a springtime Japanese holiday. "Are you sure?" she asked Papa in Japanese, while smoothing the doll's garment. "My grandfather gave it to me."

"We can't take chances," Papa said. Snatching it away, he wrapped it in newspaper and put it into a box with all the rest.

The following night, Papa drove to the dump. We looked around and saw no one there. I helped take the boxes out of the car. With only the moonlight to see by, Papa dug a shallow grave and set the boxes inside. He closed his eyes and stood very still for several minutes. Then he covered the boxes with sand. I prayed, too.

But there was more. Before the FBI agents came to our cleaners, Papa remembered the books and magazines in the closet. He brought out the dusty boxes, and said to Mama, in Japanese, "We've got to get rid of these, too." They took everything into the bathroom. While Mama tore out pages, Papa flushed them down the toilet. But if he hurried and put in too much, the toilet overflowed, and Mama would have to mop up the dirty water.

Rok-san panicked too. He destroyed all of his films, reel upon reel of eight-millimeter film in silver cans, pictures of whatever had taken his fancy, parties, picnics, birthdays. He had scenes of riding the ferry across the bay, the building of the Golden Gate and Bay Bridges, the Fair on Treasure Island, parades and other community celebrations. But the film we enjoyed most was of Papa reeling in a large striped bass in Technicolor. Papa would ask to see it frequently and *Rok-san* enjoyed showing it.

While *Rok-san* threaded film through the projector, Papa would say, "That fish was waiting to be caught." *Rok-san* would smile and joke, "*Soh.* If it hadn't been for my camera, that fish might have been swimming somewhere else in the ocean." *Rok-san* was as proud of this film as he was of all the others.

The film began with a lone sea gull, a mere speck of a bird flying lazily over the ocean against a hazy sky. There was no sound except for the clickety clicks of film advancing through the sprockets. The gull dove straight down, past the clouds, and with a tiny splash, the bird was up and away. Where the sky and water met, the film moved horizontally and faded into the land to a sandy beach with footprints washed away in the receding tide.

Farther down, along a frothy, bubbly edge, stood a solitary figure: Papa. In chest-high waders, he held a fishing rod with the butt end pointed toward the breakers. He was wearing an old Stetson hat. Behind him, a pole length away, trailed a line with a sinker and leader hooked with sardines. The sardines bounced and the sinker plowed through the shallow water, creating a tail spray.

Wading slowly, Papa was waist deep in water. He lifted the rod over his head and whipped it, the sinker, leader, and sardines sailed over the advancing breakers and disappeared.

Racing backward, he locked the reel, set the bottom of his pole into the cup of the leather harness strapped to his waist, and waved. His eyes were hidden behind sunglasses. He waited. Suddenly, the tip of his rod quivered.

Papa jumped up from watching the film. "When tip moving . . ." he told everyone excitedly, the shadow of his arm partially covering the screen.

And in the dark, *Rok-san* asked, "Do you want to go back?"

"No, no," Papa laughed, and returned to his seat.

On the screen, Papa lowered his rod, gently, and waited. "Sometime fish only tasting," he would tell us. "If no hungry, wait. Be patient. Give line, but no let line loose. When fish bite, pull, set hook."

At this point in the film, Papa stepped back and hauled back hard. The rod was bent and dipped down while its tip bobbed.

Now Papa was reeling. When he reached the water's edge, he was still reeling, but had lowered the pole. Drawing it vertical again, he reeled once more.

Finally, a fish flapped wildly in the shallow water. Its scales reflected the light. He beckoned to where I was standing off camera. I moved into the picture; he handed me the pole and ran to the water. Grabbing the fish near its gill, he dragged it up onto the beach.

Such a happy ending. Standing next to Papa, I was cradling the fish proudly. He looked down and began to laugh: I had bent the fish into a U.

When the lights came on, Papa would always ask, "Why you making fish look so small?"

"I don't know," I would reply. "That was the only way I could lift it." And everyone laughed, both onscreen and off.

Rok-san sold his cameras and equipment before the FBI came to his cleaners. He even sold his projector. But worst of all, he destroyed his films. "I had so many pictures," he told Papa and Mama, with a heavy voice. "They could have gotten us into trouble. I had pictures of the Japanese Consulate, the Japanese Pavilion at the World's Fair, pictures of the newspaper editor and his family, the annual prefectural picnic, our bishop, so many pictures on so many reels. . . I didn't have time to sort through them. I had no idea when the FBI would come. I was afraid for Asaye and the baby."

He looked at Papa, nervously , . . I cut them into strips," he continued, in a trembling voice, "And torched them in the yard in a large can. Some of them crackled. It was almost like the fourth of July." He tried to laugh.

"But thick smoke rose from my yard. I was worried about what the neighbors saw. After I was through, I realized what I had done. In a few minutes our memories, everything, had vanished, p-f-f-u-u, just like that . . . smoke . . . " His eyes misted with tears.

Papa said, "U-u-w-a-h . . ." slowly.

Several days after Christmas, Mr. Goldberg came to our cleaners. "I think it's terribly unfair," he said, while sitting at our kitchen table.

"Government no like Japanese," Papa sighed.

"Where will you go?" Mr. Goldberg said, surveying the half-packed boxes on the floor.

"Maybe go Stockton," Papa said. He looked toward Mama who was cooking dinner. "My wife's papa, he have hotel. He say, maybe Stockton better." He bent down to pick up a spoon on the floor, and said, "I scare driving San Francisco. I think maybe soldier make mistake – shoot me."

"You know, Mr. *Omi*, I received a letter from my mother last week. She's trying to get out of Berlin." Mr. Goldberg dabbed his nose with a handkerchief.

"Why she leaving?"

"She's escaping, just like you," he said, stuffing the handkerchief back into his pocket.

"Why . . . ?"

"Hitler doesn't like Jews."

"He no like Jewish?" Papa said.

"He's the Devil, Mr. *Omi*." Changing the subject, he turned to Mama. "Mmm, what's in the oven? It sure smells good. "

"Chicken," Mama said, "Chicken teriyaki. I have to be careful not to turn the gas up too high." She adjusted the dial.

"It's different with beef," Mr. Goldberg said. "I like my meat rare, not too well done." His gold tooth twinkled as he smiled.

"You know, Mr. Goldberg," Papa said, "I no can take Stockton, everything."

"Of course not."

"You like radio? Gilfillan. I show you."

Mr. Goldberg followed Papa into the living room. He motioned for Mr. Goldberg to be seated while he turned the radio on.

"What will you do with your business?" Mr. Goldberg asked.

"I no know. I try to sell, but very hard to find someone to buy. "

"My goodness," Mr. Goldberg said, "What a fine radio. I can hear the voices clearly."

"I sell cheap if you buy "

"I'll tell you what. Why don't I keep it until you get back? You're planning to return aren't you?"

"Maybe no come back," Papa said, "But okay. You keep."

"You be sure to let me know when you are leaving. I might be able to sell it for a good price in the meantime."

"*U-wahhh*, thank you, Mistah Goldberg. You like drink?" Papa walked back to the kitchen.

"No thank you, Mr. *Omi*. I have a few errands to run. I'll return for the radio tonight. Is that all right with you?"

"Yes-u," Papa said, "Thank you very much."

After Mr. Goldberg left, Papa said, "Mistah Goldberg . . . he nice man."

When the two FBI agents came to our cleaners, the short agent said to Papa, "From the FBI, sir," and held open his wallet for Papa to see. For several days, they went in and out of our cleaners to their car. And at the end of the day they would leave and return the following morning. Papa would tell Mama, in Japanese, "I don't know what they are looking for but they're sure taking their time about it."

At one point, Papa joked with the agents and offered them a drink. The short agent said, "Sure, Mr. *Omi*, why not? But the drinks are on me." They left for the bar down the street. When they came back, Papa was drunk and the short agent said to Mama," Your husband says you have a weapon in the house."

Mama looked startled at first. "N-o-o," she said in a high voice. Then she seemed to remember. She went into the kitchen and returned with a carving knife. "Is this what you mean?" she said politely to the agent.

"No, Ma'am," he said. "Please put that away before someone gets hurt."

The two men continued searching through clothes racks, under the bed, in the closets, dresser drawers, but couldn't find anything, since Papa had buried in the sand or flushed down the toilet whatever they could find that might have been incriminating.

"Sorry to have disturbed you," the tall agent said politely.

After they left, Papa was relieved. "I thought they would find something to arrest me for," he said in Japanese.

Bob Brilliant came into our cleaners a week before we left. When he came in, I wanted to surprise him. I wanted to say, *"Gunkan, gunkan, gunkan,"* as he always had said to me, but I knew it was wrong.

Instead, I said, "I like your uniform, Brilliant-san."

"You do? Good. It's a tight fit," he said, pulling down on his trousers.

"When you join Navy, Brilliant-san?" Papa asked.

"In July, *Omi-san* . . . but I didn't think it would come to this. What am I going to do now?" he said.

"You no worry. America no have navy. You be all right, you see."

"No. There's still a fleet in the Pacific. I may have to join them soon. I'm scared, *Omi-san*."

"You no worry, Brilliant-san" Papa said, earnestly. "You listen to speech? President Roosevelt say America strong. He say America win."

"I hope he's right, *Omi-san*. What are you going to do?" he asked.

"Maybe we go Stockton," Papa said. "Maybe I see you after war, Brilliant-san. Maybe I no can beat you no more. You read book get too strong, hah, hah, hah..."

"Goodbye, *Omi-san*, and thank you for being like a father." His eyes brimmed with tears. Doffing his cap, he quickly turned and walked out the door. And that was the last we saw of Brilliant-san.

Toward the end of January, with air raid drills, notices being posted all over the city, and Japanese fleeing the city, it was difficult for Papa to sit still. Finally, he told *Rok-san* on the phone in Japanese, "There's too much happening around here. San Francisco is a military area. We should move to Stockton. Everyone is leaving."

Papa had already spoken to *Ojii-san* and had asked him if he would take them in. "Of course," *Ojii-san*, had said. "We have lots of room here at the hotel. Send whatever you have by Railway Express and we will keep it here for you."

Papa and *Rok-san* tried to sell their cleaners, but couldn't find any buyers. Finally, through the cleaning plant, they found people who were interested in taking over the business but not in buying it. "I understand your problem, Mr. *Omi*," the man said smoothly, "but with this war, who knows what will happen?"

"All right," Papa said at last, "you come tomorrow, I show you books, everything. You take over next Saturday. We go Sunday."

Rok-san and *Obasan* did the same with their cleaners. When we went to see them, *Obasan* was folding clothes into a steamer trunk and *Rok-san* was sorting furniture. "If it's too large, send it by rail," Papa told them in Japanese.

"What about Henry, George, Amy and uncle *Kazuo*?" I asked. (Ben, my cousin, was in the army).

"They want to stay here and wait it out," Papa said. "Anyway, there's no room in Stockton. It would be too much to ask of your grandfather."

"Then, what about *Poochie*?" I said.

Rok-san looked sadly at her. "*Poochie*," he said, shaking his head, "No...she'd be in the way."

"Let me ask them." Papa said. "My father-in-law has two dogs."

"No, no, they are doing too much already," *Obasan* said, setting *Takashi* down on a blanket.

Rok-san said: "And I can't trust her with *Hakujins. Poochie* is Japanese. The other night someone threw tomatoes at our store from the back of a truck. Nearly broke the show window. I think they were high school boys. No, she won't like them either. ."

After we left that night, *Rok-san* decided what to do. He told us the following morning when we met him to leave for Stockton. "It usually takes fifteen minutes from here to the dump," he said, "But it took longer last night, I stopped twice. I wanted to turn back both times and then decided not to. And when I got there, the place was deserted. I didn't see another car or truck anywhere."

He said he parked his truck near the dune where the street ended and felt the cold wind on his face when he stepped out of his truck. He heard the surf and smelt the air. Sea gulls circled and screamed overhead. He walked around the truck to the passenger side, opened the door, and waited. He called to her, but she sat still. Setting his flashlight down, he called to her again. When she wouldn't move, he took a small package wrapped in waxed paper out of his pocket. His fingers trembled while he unfolded the paper. Taking the *takuan* between his thumb and forefinger, he held it out to her. In Japanese, he whispered, "Be a good girl, *Poochie*, please."

Suddenly without warning, she leaped off the seat and onto the sandy pavement. "Good girl," he said, stroking her neck. Again, he held the *takuan* near her snout, but she wouldn't take it. Instead, she sank down, crossed her paws, and lowered her head.

"You remembered," *Rok-san* said, and stroked her again. But when he held the *takuan* close to her nose, she took the radish between her teeth and let it fall.

"*Poochie*," he said misty eyed, "It's your favorite food." Wiping away the sand, he offered it again, but she wouldn't take it. Then he said, "Take care of yourself, *Poochie*. Remember Mama and I still love you. You have to stay here. You mustn't follow."

He climbed in his truck and started the engine. As he drove away, he watched her through his rear view mirror, and swore that she was crying...

"But she didn't follow. . . " he said, "She obeyed . . ."

Chapter Eleven

Though we left *Poochie* behind, we took almost everything else to Stockton. Papa had dismantled my bike and wrapped the frame and wheels in cardboard. Mama wrapped her dishes, pots, pans, utensils and silverware in newspaper and packed them into cardboard cartons. Suits, dresses, sweaters, shirts, blouses, skirts and jackets were folded and placed into a steamer trunk with an ample supply of mothballs. And then everything, including the trunk along with a pile of boxes, was shipped to Stockton before we left. But Papa and Mama did leave a few things behind: beds, sofa, chairs, tables, dresser drawers, and lamps. What hadn't been shipped was packed into suitcases and loaded into the trunk of our car. Papa's fishing pole was too long so it went inside the car. The butt end lay on top of the rear seat back rest and the tip of the pole nearly touched the dashboard. Its entire length lay in the middle between the driver and passenger seats.

I also wondered about moving to Stockton. Papa, more than Mama, loved going to Stockton. But why? My grandmother despised him. Besides that, Stockton was in the country and Papa was a city slicker. People who lived in Stockton were farmers in overalls who owned large dogs and looked suspiciously at anyone from the city. They spoke Japanese in a strange *Osaka* dialect and spit a lot. My grandfather's hotel was riddled with spittoons. He loved cigars and left half smoked butts everywhere. His patrons played cards in the lobby. They slept upstairs, but played cards all night. *Hana* they called it, a game played with small black cards, slightly larger than dominoes, with pictures of flowers on the playing side. These bachelors played for as long as my sister and I played Monopoly. We played for hours, but the money they played for was real.

But where else could we go? With notices, soldiers, sailors, blackouts and sirens, the war was closing in on us. Everyone was leaving in a panic. Out of San Francisco, Oakland, Alameda, and San Mateo -- inland -- to places like Stockton, Fresno and Marysville. Depending on whether friends or family lived there.

The journeys to Stockton before the War had always been fun, but it seemed like forever to get there. It took four hours, eighty miles of two-lane highway at forty miles per hour. But the anticipation, the preparation: closing the cleaners early, driving to Japanese Town to shop for special food, smelling Mama's cooking while lying in bed at night all made it worthwhile. To awaken in the morning to the smell of coffee, putting on a clean shirt and trousers, still warm from ironing were memorable moments. Stockton was special, a faraway castle away from home.

Papa and Mama didn't argue about when to go. Papa would decide when, but Mama wasn't always happy. "Didn't we just go?" she would say.

"It's been a month," Papa would say. "Tell your mother we're coming."

And Mama would return to the sewing machine with a harried look, as though she had burned a pot of rice.

Papa would complain frequently that my grandmother didn't like him.

And Mama would say, unperturbed, "She doesn't trust you."

"Why not?" he would say in Japanese. "I am an honest man."

"She thinks you want their money. Remember when our car broke down, and you wanted my father's car?"

Papa laughed. "That piece of junk? I only asked because it was rusty. I would have had to pay a mechanic a lot of money to fix it. Your mother," he said, shaking his head, "I'll never understand her. She doesn't trust anyone, not even you."

And Mama looked away without a word and I understood.

Papa enjoyed the hotel. He spoke to boarders as though he owned it. He often joined in card games. If he lost, he'd say, "I never play again. They too smart." But if he won, "I lucky," he'd say, "I take all money. 'I sorry, I say,' but they no believe. I no like to take money.'"

Mama quietly forgave Papa. She had her own unspoken feelings. But she never told him. She only told *Shii-chan* and me. Her mother had never loved her.

After crossing the bay in a ferry, my stomach would feel queasy. I'd get over this feeling when we began to see farms and low-lying hills. Sometimes we'd see cows and horses. Papa drove fast, faster than the speed limit, but he'd watch the mirror for policemen on motorcycles

My mind would drift while we were on the road. The highway was endless. I'd struggle to keep my eyes open while the radio faded in and out. But suddenly I'd awake to static, scratchy, unnerving, like a phonograph needle gone awry. Music in my half sleep had become a high-pitched, tchi-i-i-i that buzzed in my ear. Papa would fuss with the dial and the overhead lines wouldn't stop. They kept coming. Then, just when I was wide awake, Papa would coincidentally turn the radio off. With a fresh mind, I would watch for the chrome grills coming toward us down the highway. I knew most every car by model and make. I made it a game to see who could remember first. After a while, Papa would give up, "You too good," he would say and I would feel proud.

My grandfather's hotel boarded Japanese men year around. Even in the off-season. My grandfather was a contractor. He put laborers together with farmers and received a commission. Mama also told us that men of all ages would come off the boat in San Francisco seeking work and a roof over their heads.

Mama said that these men would come to Stockton on the train and that her father would pick them up at the station and bring them to the hotel. Mama and her mother cleaned their rooms and fed them. But after 1924, with the new immigration law, Japanese couldn't come to America anymore. Though her father once had a lot of farm laborers in the hotel, they became fewer each year because of the new law.

"And with the Depression everything got worse," Mama said. "But by then I was married and my father was rich. It was hard for him not to be able to find work for his men. Many left to find other work, but many also stayed."

When we came upon Burma Shave signs -- single words on sign posts spaced along the highway that collectively formed a phrase, like "Shave –Faster – Without – Disaster" -- on our way to Stockton, *Shii-chan* and I would read them aloud, making Mama and Papa laugh. Without realizing it, we had become like every other family traveling in cars. Sometimes Papa would say, "Only in America we can enjoy like this. In Japan, only *kane mochi*, the rich, have car. But no need car in Japan," he would add without bitterness. "You know why . . . ?" he would continue, "In Japan I go anywhere -- no shame, no embarrassing. In America, only in car, I can enjoy same way."

After Livermore, I would begin to nod. Warm air filled the car. By the time we reached Tracy, I would be asleep. When Papa finally parked in front of the hotel, I would wake up hot and sticky. Then I would remember: this is Stockton, not San Francisco.

My memories of the hotel are still vivid. I can recall the deserted streets bordering the hotel, picture the relics in the dusty driveway -- Model T Fords, Chevrolets, Plymouths, rusted trucks, carriages sitting idle, covered with dust and cobwebs. Even the olive trees looked tired. I often wondered whether they were alive. They were my grandmother's. She would pick them clean every year and pickle the olives in Mason jars and give them away to relatives and friends. I never liked her green olives; I preferred them dark and ripe.

We usually went in and out of the hotel from its side, through a squeaky screen door since the front doors were hard to open. They had to be pushed. Unsuspecting guests sometimes stumbled into the lobby, where elderly men would look up from their card games and smile.

But I was frightened of my grandfather's dogs. He kept them tied to ropes near the screen door. The two dogs would come out from the basement below the landing. Whenever we got too close, they would snarl and growl. Strands of saliva would drip from their mouths. They were German Shepherds. If my grandfather saw them in time, he would yell in Japanese, "Down, down, down, get down," and if they didn't obey, he would kick one or both dogs, until they yelped and went into the basement.

"Don't mind them," he would say, while tugging on a suspender. "They only bite *Hakujins*."

And now with the war, this would be our final journey to Stockton. On the morning of moving day, the *Hakujin* couple who had taken over our cleaners arrived early. It was raining. They helped us load the car and gave us a bag of donuts for our journey. Even Papa had to admit that they were nice people after all.

Papa stopped at the service station for gasoline on the way to *Rok-san's* cleaners. If it hadn't been for the rain, it was as though we were going to the beach with Papa's fishing pole between us. While the wiper blades swished back and forth, I wondered whether *Shii-chan* and I would go to school in Stockton. I also wondered what Papa, Mama, *Rok-san* and *Obasan* would do, now that they'd given up their cleaners. I'd often heard Papa and Mama talking about Stockton, and knew that Papa didn't like *Obaa-san*.

But Papa said, "We have much better chance in Stockton."

"Why?" Mama asked, in Japanese. She didn't think it was a good idea to move, either.

"Wait and see," said Papa. "This war has only begun. If Japan invades California, we will be safer in Stockton."

It felt strange to be leaving, knowing that we might never return. Mama told *Shii-chan* that we were only moving temporarily. "I'd rather live in San Francisco," *Shii-chan* pouted. "I hate Stockton." It wasn't until she saw *Rok-san* and *Obasan* that she perked up. She was happy to see that they were traveling with us. She kept looking back to wave. She couldn't wait to touch the baby.

Finally, we stopped near Tracy. We parked on a shoulder under a line of trees. Cars went by in both directions. "We sure picked a bad day," Papa said in Japanese through a mouthful of rice.

"At least it stopped raining," *Rok-san* said with a burp. Mama offered *Obasan* a plate but she wouldn't take it. She smiled instead.

"How is *Takashi*?" Mama asked.

"Fine," *Obasan* said, softly. "His rash is almost gone."

"Can I hold him?" Shii-chan asked.

"*Oi . . .*" *Rok-san* interrupted, "You'd better eat something now," he said, "There won't be time once we get there."

"I'll eat while you're driving, Daddy," she said. *Obasan* now called *Rok-san,* "Daddy," instead of *anata*, the polite word for you.

To *Shii-chan, Obasan* said quietly, "Maybe after we get to Stockton, okay?" She smiled.

When Papa turned onto Lafayette Street, he asked Mama for the time. "Quarter past four," she said in Japanese.

"We're late," he said irritably, as though it were her fault. "I told your father we'd be here at three."

"It doesn't matter," Mama said, combing *Shii-chan's* hair. "Not in this weather. It's not as if they're waiting."

"Do we have rooms in the hotel?" I asked.

"No . . " Mama said. She pointed to the house on the other side of the driveway. "*Asoko*, there. . . Your grandmother said there."

"It looks spooky," I said. I hadn't noticed this house before. The porch was slanted and pickets were missing from the front fence. A tangle of blackberries and flowers grew in a heap.

And then, Papa said, "This rain is not going to let up." He stepped out of the car and signaled for *Rok-san* and *Obasan* to join us, and said to us, "We'd better let them know we're here," and motioned for us to get out too.

When we stepped inside the hotel, I heard a familiar sound -- a rapid patter from the kitchen. *Obaa-san* was chopping vegetables with a cleaver. "*Maa*, you've grown since I last saw you!" she said to me in Japanese. "Do you still like ice cream?" When I shook my head, no, she wiped her hands on her apron and said, "Yes, yes, you and *Shii-chan* like ice cream. Come, come, follow me." It was just like old times.

Ojii-san sat on a stool hunched over a bowl of noodles.

"Where are your dogs?" I asked politely.

Dipping chopsticks into a bowl, he sucked and slurped noodles into his mouth. "They're gone," he said in Japanese.

"Gone?" I said.

"Gone. . . buried over there." He pointed out the window toward the rear of the hotel.

"What happened?" I asked. I thought of *Poochie*.

Instead of answering me, he turned to Mama and said, "No one makes *udon* noodles as good as your mother. Wiping his mouth with the back of his hand, he said to Mama, *"Mo, ipai kure*. Bring me another bowl." And then, to me, he said, in Japanese, "Someone clubbed them to death."

"Wha-at?" I said.

"They were dead when I came out to feed them this morning."

"Who would do such a thing?" I asked.

"*Hakujins*," he said. "They took the silverware in the basement and left the two by four."

Mama picked up his bowl and went into the kitchen, when *Obaa-san* came out. She took *Shii-chan's* hand and beckoned me to follow her. While Mama poured broth over *Ojii-san's* noodles in the kitchen, *Obaa-san* opened the icebox door and poked around inside. She brought out two cardboard boxes and said to Shii-chan and I with a smile, "Orange or chocolate?"

I still couldn't believe what happened.

Ojii-san called to me from the dining room. "*Minoru*, come here."

He sat me down on a chair and said in Japanese, "Those dogs were useless. They didn't do their job. . ."

"Useless . . . ?" I said. "But they were only dogs . . ."

"Yes, they were only dogs," he repeated, ". . . Only dogs, but they let those miserable *Hakujins* get away."

And I thought . . . *but they were only dogs*.

While *Shii-chan* and I ate flavored ice on sticks, we saw Papa and *Ojii-san* walking past the window. We hurried outside and followed them to the house. Moving into this house now was exciting.

"This place needs work," *Ojii-san* said. He pushed open the creaky door. "But it's much better than the hotel. "

"*Soh*, "said Papa, in Japanese, "It is more quiet here."

"You won't have to go up and down stairs," *Ojiisan* said, lighting up a cigar. "You also have your own bathroom," he added.

"How long do you think we'll be here?" I asked, in English.

"For as long as you like," *Ojii-san* said, in Japanese, and laughed.

"No, I mean, really . . ." I said, in English.

"Depends on the war," *Ojii-san* said, in Japanese. He turned to Papa and *Rok-san* and asked, "When do you think the war will be over?"

"The Japanese navy is winning everywhere," said Papa.

"There, you see . . ." *Ojii-san* said. "But you can stay here even after the war is over."

"What's that smell?" Papa asked. *Rok-san* pinched his nose and looked around.

Ojii-san laughed. "*Tsukemono*. Pickles," he said and led us into the kitchen.

"*U-w-a-h*," Papa said. "Look at that." Large ceramic jars with wooden lids covered most of the floor. I continued holding my nose and *Ojii-san* chuckled.

Rok-san shook his head. Fanning his face, he exclaimed loudly about the smell, "*Ku-sai, kusai... mataku kusai!*"

Ojii-san roared with laughter. "We will serve these to the soldiers if they should ever get this far." And they all laughed. Then Papa, *Rok-san*, uncle John, and *Ojii-san* carried the jugs to the shed.

The War had taken a toll on the lives of the Japanese immigrant men who were still single. They had not been able to earn enough money to return to Japan nor find a life in America. It was depressing to see such men drinking and gambling in the hotel. I'd never paid much attention to them before the war. They were a sorry bunch, always playing cards with Bull Durham cigarettes dangling from their lips. Papa said they were gamblers. But when Mama told me about their plight I felt sorry. She said that when she first came to the hotel in 1917, they were hard-working young men. "Your grandfather kept their names in a ledger and hired them out to farmers in French Camp and Lodi. We had forty to fifty men, sometimes more. The hotel was always full. They were hopeful of making a fortune and returning home. New immigrants came nearly every week. Women too. But then the law changed and women couldn't come any more; later on, men couldn't come either. Some made it back to Japan with a few dollars, but many died penniless. *Ojii-san* buried them in the Stockton cemetery or sent their ashes home."

"What will happen to them?" I asked.

"I don't know," said Mama. "They've been in America too long. It's hard for them to change now."

"Will they stay in America even if Japan wins the war?" I asked.

"Once anyone has been in America for as long as they have, it's hard to go home. Everything changes if you've been away that long," she said. "Your father can tell you how hard it was for him. Even people change with time. When you grow older, you'll understand what I mean . . ."

Chapter Twelve

"Maybe we should have stayed in San Francisco," Papa said to Mama, and she seemed to agree. "I hate working in the hotel every day, she said. "It's just like what I had to do when I first came to America from Japan." But by May, our fate was sealed. Temporary and permanent centers were being built for Japanese in California and in other states. By late April, families, aliens and citizens alike, were being transported to Tanforan, Merced and Manzanar. We would soon go to the Stockton Assembly Center.

Our three-month stay in Stockton was like a dream when compared to the nightmare of air raid sirens, arrests, burials and burnings in San Francisco. Papa and *Rok-san* seemed to enjoy the leisure. They'd never spent a day in their life without working. To add to their pleasantry, Papa and *Rok-san* built a ping-pong table using a sheet of four by eight plywood and sawhorses. I played after school and on the weekends. The sound of paddle to ball and ball to table, clack, clack, clack . . . clack, clack . . . clack, clack, combined with laughter and cajoling resonated in the driveway. Papa and *Rok-san* loved to play, but they weren't very good. I let them beat themselves.

School in Stockton was only three blocks away. I met many Asians from families in the neighborhood. But I'd felt odd to be among them, as though I was from another culture, even though we were all *Nisei*.

Shii-chan and I would often play dominoes or monopoly with Papa. We would play until Mama began setting the table for dinner. He got excited whenever he got Boardwalk and Park Place. He would build hotels and eagerly await our pieces. If we passed "GO" and collected two hundred dollars, he would clap, laugh, and say, "*U-u-w-a-a*, you lucky."

Rok-san and *Obasan* were at ease in Stockton. Though *Obasan* would still fuss with snacks and insist on cooking or do the dishes, *Takashi* kept her busy with diaper changes and nursing. If Mama were to cook, *Obasan* would insist on doing the dishes, unless *Takashi* interrupted. She and Mama seemed to get along well, although Mama spent more time in the hotel, instead of with us.

Our routine was quickly broken when the evacuation notices were posted. It was as if a judge had passed sentence; we were all going to jail. Though no one seemed surprised with the verdict, everyone wondered about the sentence. We had to get rid of everything except for what we could take in suitcases. We were destined for the Stockton Fairgrounds.

"Stockton Fairgrounds? Where's that?" It seemed like everyone in Stockton knew but us.

It was as if we were going on a picnic. "We take . . . toothpaste, toilet paper, soap, matches, what else do we need?" Papa would ask in Japanese.

When Ojii-san learned about the evacuation order, he threw his magnifying glass on the floor. "Why?" he roared in Japanese. "We haven't done anything wrong!" Picking up a chair, he smashed it against a table. Then he threw a stool across the room, shattering the dinner plates that were stacked on the table. "What will happen to this hotel?" he shouted.

Obaa-san and Mama heard the noise from the kitchen. So did I. I was in the lobby. "What's going on in here?" *Obaa-san* said, in Japanese, with a soup ladle in her hand. Mama stood behind her with a towel and a frying pan. When *Ojii-san* turned and kicked the counter, "*Obaa-san* said, in a quieter voice, ". . . Have you been drinking again?"

"No, Ma," said Uncle John from across the room, "I just gave him the news."

"He didn't know . . .?" Mama said in Japanese, setting down the pan.

"Didn't know what?" *Obaa-san* asked.

"The evacuation order," Uncle John said, "We have to move. The army is clearing us out of here." *Obaa-san* nodded as if she understood and went back into the kitchen. Uncle John wrapped an arm around *Ojii-san's* neck, and led him out of the dining room. "*Otoo-san*," he said softly, "Take it easy."

Papa, *Rok-san* and Uncle John had already sold their cars to the used car dealer the day before. I'd felt devastated. The world around us was closing in. Our ship was sinking. The following day, they discarded everything else, even the pickles. And though the jars were now empty, the smell was unmistakable -- putrid miso. Electric fans hummed and twirled, but the thermometer read eighty-five. Mama and *Obaa-san* fanned their faces, while Papa, Uncle John and *Rok-san* mopped their brows with handkerchiefs. With nothing for us to do, *Shii-chan* and I played with folding fans, flipping them this way and that, and watched.

In and out they went, stopping only to fan or wipe their faces. *Ojii-san* had left it to Uncle John to decide what to sell in the hotel: tables, chairs, radios, bedding, bottles of *shoyu*, boxes of canned foods, sacks of rice, dresses, suits and trousers on hangers, shoes, hats, lamps, sofas, bed-frames, and on and on, so much came out of the hotel. What couldn't be stored in the basement sat on the sidewalk. Papa and *Rok-san* had our things on display too.

"Not my bike. . ." I said to Papa, putting down my fan. "It's still new."

"No can take," Papa said, leaning my Schwinn against a table.

"Why not?"

"Government no allow," he said, toweling his face.

"Can't it go in the basement?"

"Already too full," he said, "I buy you bicycle when war is over."

Dusty trucks lined the street outside the hotel. Strangers poked at clothing, ran fingers over the dining room table, pulled dishes out of boxes, sat on sofas and chairs, lifted off lamp shades, looked for price tags. An unshaven man stroked my bike. Curling his fingers around the handlebar, he tooted the horn and turned the front light off and on. "I'll give you a dollar for it," he said.

"Three dollars!" Papa said loudly.

"You drive a hard bargain, mister. I'll give you two." When Papa nodded, the man handed him two one-dollar bills. Stomping on his cigarette, he picked up the bike and loaded it into the back of his truck. I stood and watched while the truck disappeared around the corner.

The next day Papa, Mama, *Rok-san, Obasan, Shii-chan* and I stood with hundreds of other families in front of the Buddhist church, while soldiers in khaki colored uniforms, wearing steel helmets, pointed rifles at us. *Ojii-san, Obaa-san* and Uncle John were not with us, because Uncle John had been saying goodbyes to his *Hakujin* friends.

Though the soldiers looked ominous, I felt comfortable because there were so many Japanese with us. And yet, uncertainty charged the air. Everyone looked nervous. *Takashi* was crying and *Obasan* cuddled him. It was as if we were headed for disaster, like the gas chamber or the electric chair, until finally, we boarded the bus. Once inside, it was as though we entered a capsule, quiet, insulated from the outside. Even Takashi stopped crying.

It took less than fifteen minutes to get to the fairgrounds. Once we arrived, we poured out of the buses onto a stubbly field. The soldiers in uniform, wearing soft hats, directed us to put suitcases, duffel bags, boxes and bundles in a pile. I was glad that Mama had sewn "*Omi*" tightly on everything: sheets, pillowcases and towels bore our names. Papa had stenciled our suitcases as well. But we all looked silly wearing labels, long cardboard tags with numbers that matched our baggage.

Papa, Mama, and *Rok-san* stood in line near the grandstand, while *Obasan, Shii-chan* and I waited near the pile. The afternoon air smelled like a farm, like uncle *Kazuo's* chicken ranch in Petaluma. With so many of us bunched together, it felt like a picnic. But the soldiers with rifles looked uneasy. And why not? They were outnumbered. The comfort I'd felt, had meant uneasiness for them. But they held tightly to their rifles. I wondered whether they were loaded. A few were aimed at us.

We huddled in small groups, while the soldiers searched suitcases, cardboard boxes, bundles and bags. Someone said that the soldiers were looking for contraband, anything suspicious, radios, cameras, anything that could be used by spies. Spies? I thought. Could there be a spy among us? Papa had a radio but he wasn't a spy. And *Rok-san* once owned a camera. Besides, the FBI had already searched our homes.

"Does anyone know how long they're keeping us here?" someone asked.

"For the duration . . ." someone replied.

"No . . . this place is temporary," another voice said, and added, "If the war should last that long."

Takashi was crying again, but this time he wouldn't stop. *Obasan* tried to comfort him while the soldiers kept searching. Finally, she unbuttoned her blouse and nursed him without hesitation. Her duty was to her baby, and the soldiers looked the other away. "That's all he wanted," *Rok-san* laughed. "He was hungry." He took the diaper bag from *Obasan*, and told Papa to go ahead.

After filling out forms, Mama unpinned the tag from my shirt and we walked toward the parking lot. We followed people who seemed to know the way. Arrows on the signs pointed everywhere.

"What number are you looking for?" people would say and then, "Really, where's that?"

"That way, I think," a man would guess.

Papa kept saying, "We in two. . ." so we looked for a sign that said two.

"There it is. . ." I saw it first. The number "two" was painted in black on a white board.

"That's not a house, that's a. . . a . . ." *Shii-chan* said.

"Barrack, like what soldiers sleep in." I said. By now, her whining disturbed me.

"We're not soldiers," Shii-chan continued.

"We don't have a choice," I said, a bit loudly, "We have to go where they tell us to."

"But I don't want to live in a . . a. . . barrack," she said, tearfully, "I want to go home."

"You're tired, *Shii-chan*," *Obasan* said, comfortingly, "Just like *Takashi*. You need to rest and sleep."

When we stepped inside our unit, I looked for a door, and said, "Where's the bathroom?"

"The soldier said, 'Near the big tent,'" Mama said.

"Out there?" I whined, sounding a bit like Shii-chan.

"Yes . . ." Mama said, surveying our room. And then to Papa, she said, "We don't have a sink . . ."

I interrupted. "I'm going to the bathroom. I can't wait. "

"*Chotto*. Wait a minute," Papa said, impatiently, "We looking place over."

"What's to look over?" I said. "I've gotta go."

Mama moved the suitcases over near the wall while Papa walked to the wood stove in the middle of the room. "Stockton Record . . ." he said, and tossed the newspaper back into the stove.

"I wonder where my parents are?" Mama said nervously in Japanese.

"We'll see them later," Papa said reassuringly. "We'd better go to the toilet now."

"I have to go too," *Shii-chan* said.

After we stepped outside, Mama asked Papa, "Did they give you a key?"

"No, just close the door," Papa said, "Everyone here is Japanese."

Like the soldier said, the bathroom was near the tent. Papa and I stood alongside an elderly man and peed into a trough. The man drew in deeply on a cigarette and shook himself. I hated the mingled smell of urine and cigarette smoke. He waited until we were through, then flushed the trough from his end and tossed the cigarette into a can.

We washed in an adjoining room where the sinks came up to my chest. I could see the showerheads in the adjoining room. "Is that where we bathe?" I asked.

"Yes," Papa said. "But no tub."

No tub? I'd never showered in my life.

We waited for Mama and *Shii-chan* near the woodpile, while a man with a dirty face carried buckets of coal into the room between the bathrooms. Papa said the coal was for the furnace. "Big boiler," he said. While we watched the man stoke coal, Mama came out with *Shii-chan*. "They don't have partitions between the toilets," she complained.

Papa laughed. "At least they no outside."

Mama didn't think he was funny.

We stood in line to eat. We had to wait until everyone with white tags had eaten -- we had blue tags, since we were among the last to register. They gave us a metal tray, cup, knife, fork and spoon. I was hungry and the line was long. The men who stood in front of me had red tags. When they got to the door, a man waved them off and said they would have to wait their turn until after the blue tags. The men grumbled about how long they waited and how confusing the tags were. When we finally got inside the mess hall, the people with white tags who had finished eating left through a different door.

Men and women in aprons scrubbed pots and pans while we moved toward the counter. Others lugged containers of steaming food. A man in a T-shirt behind the counter placed a patty on my plate, and joked in Japanese with people in line. "Chew it real well," he said to me in Japanese with a wink of an eye. I smiled and nodded yes.

The meat smelled good. So did the boiled potato and carrots. Mama took a slice of bread from a tray and put it on top of my patty. I couldn't wait to eat. We followed Papa to an empty table scattered with crumbs. Mama carefully brushed them into a paper napkin. Diners on the next table ate with their fingers. One woman laughed loudly and the man next to her pounded the table and guffawed. Mama told us these people were from a different part of Japan; I didn't understand their dialect, though Mama and Papa did. Papa spoke to them in his dialect and they nodded their heads.

When I began to eat, the unpleasant events of the day vanished. But when I dropped my fork and stooped to pick it up, I saw the guard tower and my stomach tightened again.

Mama poured us all glasses of Kool-Aid from a pitcher. *Shii-chan* picked at her food, and stared at diners with wide eyes. Papa spoke loudly to the strange man and woman at the next table. And then I heard a man at the end of our table say, "This is what I used to feed my dog." His friend laughed, and said, "My dog got better than this."

I didn't care what they thought. I cleaned my plate and went back for seconds.

After dinner, we stopped at the woodpile for logs. "If cold tonight, I make fire," Papa told us. He shredded newspapers and placed them under the kindling in the stove. Mama tacked bed sheets on the windows and set a wash pan on a wooden crate. She told us to spit into the white bucket on the floor when we brushed our teeth. "The green can is for fresh water," she said and shook it to make sure it was full. And this was our new beginning. This was what we had to get used to for as long as the war was being fought. It was like moving from the city to the country, except that this country had a fence around it.

But we weren't as bad off as some of the others. We were lucky not to be in a horse stable. "*Uchida-san* said he found manure under the paint," Papa said.

"That poor man," said Mama. "He was the cleanest boarder in our hotel. He kept his room clean."

"I think they put all the bachelors into the stables," Papa said, as if bachelors were outcasts.

"No," I said. "I saw a boy with his mother and father."

"*Honto*? Really?" Mama said.

"Yes," said *Shii-chan*, "So did I."

"*U-wahhh*, we lucky then," Papa said.

"Lucky?" Mama said, wearily in Japanese. "We don't have anywhere to hang our clothes, we have to go outside to eat, we don't have our own bathroom and we can hear everything they say in the next room." Papa pointed at the wall and placed his finger to his lips. He didn't want everyone to hear Mama complain.

The partitions were paper-thin. I could hear whispering from next-door, which annoyed me. I couldn't sleep. I lay in bed, covering my ears, and counted knots in the ceiling. Now and then a beam of light from the tower would brighten our room. In the middle of counting, three hundred and one, three hundred and two, I heard a pounding on the wall. Papa stood in shorts near the wall, and shouted, "*Oi, damate kure yo*! Be quiet in there!" The whispering stopped, and I felt relief, until I heard the crickets chirping outside.

I awoke to a clanging noise. It sounded like a fire drill. "Breakfast is ready," Mama said quietly. The sounds came from a metal triangle suspended near the mess hall door. Before every meal, a man in an apron struck it with a metal rod. "Two clangs means it's our turn," Mama said.

I wore the clothes I'd worn the day before. At first, I didn't know where we were. The sun came in through the window and Papa was lathering his face with soap. He was getting ready to shave. Mama was wiping *Shii-chan's* face with a towel and helping her put on a dress. The floor was cold. I looked for my socks, and then found a fresh pair in my shoes.

When Mama tossed Papa's underwear on the cot, I heard a woman's voice from next door. "Wash your face before you go outside."

A little girl asked, "Where's my comb, Mama?"

"Come here and I'll help you," the woman said. I put on my trousers and hoped we wouldn't see her. Papa had spoken so harshly to her last night. I looked out our window and saw people walking toward the mess hall. Neighbors, I thought. We're all in this together and we've got to get along.

In the mess hall, Uncle John told Mama, "Pop's not well. He's been hurting and won't see a doctor."

When we went to their unit after breakfast, *Obaa-san* was praying before her *butsudan*. "*Nam myo horengeikyo, nam myo horengeikyo,*" she chanted over and over again with her eyes closed. The room smelled of incense. The wispy smoke curled out of the sand filled urn.

"Come on in and sit down," whispered Uncle John, while unfolding chairs.

"How is he?" asked Papa. *Ojii-san* was asleep on the cot.

"Not too good," he said. "He won't see a doctor . . ."

Ojii-san stirred. He rolled over and looked blankly toward us.

"How are you?" Papa said in Japanese. "How do you feel?"

Ojii-san grunted, "U-m," and turned the other way.

"We're here to see you," said Mama in Japanese. He grunted again.

"I guess we should leave . . ." Papa said.

Obaa-san continued to chant, "*Nam myo horengei kyo, nam myo horengei kyo . . .*"

"He'll be all right," Papa said, reassuringly. "He's strong."

"Thanks for coming," Uncle John said to Papa. "I thought he might listen to you."

Mama went to see him every day. "It's getting worse," she said to Papa. "And he still won't see a doctor."

Papa and everyone else in our block kept busy. No one sat around and moped. Papa helped produce plays. Before the war, he and *Rok-san* had acted in amateur productions. Their older brother *Jiro*, was well-known as a *Shinpa* actor in Japan. I never learned exactly what *Shinpa* meant. Whenever I asked Papa for an explanation, he would say, "*Shinpa*, modern, not like *Kabuki*." I gathered that they were contemporary plays about ordinary people.

My Uncle *Jiro* had come to America like *Kawakami Otojiro*, the founder of *Shinpa* theater. *Otojiro* toured America and Europe at the turn of the century. My uncle came in 1930 with a troupe of actors and toured California for six months. It was the year I was born, and it was my Uncle *Jiro* who chose my name, *Minoru*.

Papa and *Rok-san's* first production was *Chushingura*, a tale about samurai. They added sound to the film. They'd done the play many times on stage and spoke the words behind a bed sheet for a screen. They added the sound of the receding ocean tide by shifting gravel back and forth in a metal wash tub. Papa and *Rok-san* became instant celebrities. Many young men and women came to our unit to ask if they could help in future plays.

Shii-chan and I saw little of Papa and Mama during the day. While they worked, we played. We learned to look after ourselves. But during the summer I frequently wished we were back at the cleaners. I missed the Sunday drives and even school. *Shii-chan* and I would play Monopoly in the grandstand where it was cool. But after a while she would leave to play with her friends and I would sit and watch the joggers circling the track.

I sometimes played with the boys I met in school in Stockton. We played catch and marbles. Toward the end of summer, the talk in the mess hall and grandstand was that the Assembly Center was closing and that we were going to a Relocation Center. There were ten centers in all: Minidoka, Idaho; Manzanar, California; Gila River, Arizona; Amache, Colorado; Rohwer, Arkansas; Topaz, Utah; Tule Lake, California; Poston, Arizona; Heart Mountain, Wyoming, and Jerome, Arkansas. We were going to Rohwer.

"Did you hear?" I said to my friend *Hiromu*, while scribing a circle in the dirt.

"Hear what?" he said.

"We're leaving this place for Arkansas."

"Arkansas? Isn't that a state?"

"Yeah," I said, "it's in the South. Somewhere near Alabama, I think."

"Man. . . That sounds far away. Is it past Texas?"

"Oh yeah. Way past Texas."

"How are we going to get there anyway?"

"Don't ask me," I said. "Maybe Greyhound." *Hiromu* was a year younger than me, and asked even more questions than my sister.

"Do we have to go?" he asked.

"We don't have a choice. Why do you think we're in here?"

"Because we're Japanese, right?"

"Right. From now on, until the war is over, we're safer in camp. They also want us out of the way so we can't cause any trouble. "Do you want to play for keeps or funsies?" I placed five marbles in the circle.

"Keeps . . ." he said, setting his marbles next to mine.

"Go ahead and lag to see who goes first," I said, drawing a line in the dirt.

I had a good shooter, a dark agate with white swirls inside a greenish milky cloud. When I twirled it with a flick of my thumb and forefinger, a dark crimson eye whirled dead center, the other colors swirled around it.

"Wow," *Hiromu* said, "Where did you get that?"

"It was in a sack of marbles I got last Christmas."

After a half hour or so of playing, I had won all of his marbles.

"I didn't know you were <u>that</u> good," he said, looking downtrodden.

"I got lucky," I said. "Here, you can have your marbles back."

"Really? Gee, thanks . . . "

I wished that they would change their minds and let us go back home.

Mama showed Papa the notice. "It says we're leaving Stockton in three weeks," she said.

"Did everyone get one?" Papa asked.

"My parents did," Mama said.

"I'd better see if *Rokuro* got one too," Papa said, taking the notice from her.

And then Mama said, in a hushed voice, to Papa, "My father's gotten worse. My brother doesn't think he is well enough to travel."

"Your father is unhappy about losing his hotel," Papa said.

"I know . . ." said Mama.

"He has to help himself . . ." Papa said, in Japanese. "We can't change him."

"But his foot is black and blue," Mama said.

Papa is right, I thought. *Grandpa will be fine. He's just mad about losing everything that took him more than thirty years to build.*

Chapter Thirteen

The day we left the Assembly Center, I'd felt as excited as when I first rode a roller coaster at Play Land at the beach. I saw the locomotive with smoke curling out its stack. I stood behind *Shii-chan* and looked up and down the tracks at the line of cars. Our car was near the middle. We walked in single file behind other families to board it. Papa and Mama went first and helped *Shii-chan*. I grabbed the handrail and helped myself up. "All aboard . . ." the conductor shouted.

We walked down the aisle to about the middle of the car. Papa motioned me to sit next to him. Mama and *Shii-chan* sat across from us. Most everyone was busy putting things away. Hardly anyone spoke. I was afraid to ask which way we were going. In my geography book I'd seen maps of New Mexico and Arizona, and pictures of Indians with blankets, cabooses, locomotives, cowboys on horses, cacti and the desert. I thought we were traveling south. No one else seemed to care. Glumly, they stared out the window.

When we hit the desert, all I saw was mile after mile of sagebrush and cacti until we got to a train station. Then I couldn't look outside anymore; we had to pull down the shades. Suddenly, we were prisoners, being secretly transported to the back woods of Arkansas. The *Nisei* who sat in the seat in front of us said to his wife, "They say it's for our own protection! If you ask me, they're afraid. What they're doing is illegal and they don't want anyone to know about it."

"*Soh* . . ." said Papa to the man. "Maybe they no want us to see. Maybe big secret outside."

"No, Mr. *Omi*, I don't think so," said the man. "I think it's the other way around."

In the dark compartment all sounds and motions had stopped, and we had a moment of tranquility. *Shii-chan* kept sleeping and continued to sleep. I envied her. The train went forward a short distance, then jolted. We moved backward with loud screeching and banging sounds. "Changing engines," someone said. The banging continued and I wished we were moving again. Suddenly, slowly at first, we went forward, then faster, until I heard the familiar clickety-clack and the compartment began to sway from side to side again. We were on our way. And as the train knifed through the prairie, I fell asleep.

Sunlight streamed in through the window below the shade. I rubbed my eyes. Someone said we were in Texas. How could he know? The desert remained unchanged. It shimmered under the sun, baked like bread. We were rolling -- fast. Crags and bluffs, followed by bluffs and crags, one after another, running like a stream. But the sand looked too hot to touch. I perspired even with the shade drawn. Shifting on the smooth hard backed chairs, I hoped I wasn't disturbing Papa. My spine and buttocks couldn't find a soft spot. Worse yet, my underwear stuck to me like toilet paper and the heavy smoke from cigarettes made me cough. And yet, I was hungry.

We ate our meals in the dining car. It felt strange to see colored waiters dressed in starched shirts and black coats. They looked like actors from a Shirley Temple movie. We sat at small tables covered with white tablecloths and waited for food, which they brought out on trays.

"Hey, how about this . . ." someone said, "First class . . ."

"Yeah," said a second man, "Just like rich folks."

"Don't be a wise guy," another man laughed. "They'll make you wash the dishes."

We sat quietly and ate. Mama tucked a napkin under *Shii-chan's* chin while she poked at her egg with a fork. Papa and Mama drank coffee. I buttered my toast and looked out the window at the mountains. It felt good. Almost as if we were back at the cleaners again, sitting at a table together, having breakfast. Meanwhile, the train droned on.

Mama poured water into paper cups and told *Shii-chan* and me to take salt tablets to make up for the minerals we lost, while sweating. I hated its taste. "You have to," Mama insisted.

"No," I said, sounding a bit like *Shii-chan*, while she gulped hers down.

The conductor kept the windows shut despite the heat. I wanted to go to the rear and stand outside between the cars, but people stood in the aisle and waited their turn for the restroom. Mama fanned her face with a newspaper and Papa took off his shirt. Several men had taken off their shoes, which added a foul smell to the cigarette smoke. Finally, a man near the front of our compartment slid open his window. The rush of air felt cool.

"*Ah-a-a-a!*" Papa said gratefully.

But then a woman screamed suddenly, "*I-yah!*" Through the open window, soot from the locomotive flew in like black moths and clung to our skin, clothes, and hair. When I saw Papa, Mama, and *Shii-chan's* faces, I laughed until my stomach hurt.

"Look at yourself," *Shii-chan* said with a smirk. "Your face looks worse than Papa's."

"Close that window!" a woman shouted in Japanese.

The man who opened it tried, but the window wouldn't shut. But the man behind him, leaned over and released the latch. Together, they closed it.

Mama stirred when the train stopped. She rose from her seat and said she had to check on *Ojii-san*. *Shii-chan* said that she wanted to go with Mama, but Mama said no. Papa grumbled, but snapped at me instead of *Shii-chan*. "*Gasa, gasa!* You moving around too much," he said. But the harder I tried to sit still, the more uncomfortable I became. If Papa hadn't said anything everything would have been fine. Finally, I rose from my seat and worked myself past the people in the aisle. It felt cool and comfortable in the space between the cars.

That night, when the man who sat across from us set newspapers in the aisle to sleep on, I nudged Papa. But Papa had already begun to doze. Shaking his head irritably, he said, "Go to sleep."

When the lights in the compartment dimmed, the man in the aisle curled comfortably. He had an arm tucked under his head. I marveled in the darkness while the train rumbled on. Suddenly I heard a woman's voice. "*Mah... gomen-nasai.* Excuse me," she said.

And from the aisle, I heard, "*Ah, itai*! That hurts!"

When Papa turned on the light, the lady was leaning on my backrest. "*Nani o shiteru no?*" he grumbled, "What are you doing?"

Shading her eyes, she stepped back.

"*Ah itai!*" the man in the aisle said again.

"*Gomen... ne,*" the lady apologized. She stepped around him and went down the aisle.

The man picked up the newspapers and returned to his seat.

"*Baka-ja,*" Papa whispered, "He no have common sense."

The following morning Mama left several times to see *Ojii-san*. "Don't worry," Papa said in Japanese, "He'll be all right. If I were you, I'd be more worried about your mother." And then he laughed. Mama glared angrily a Papa and left.

I awoke when the train grounded to a stop. I sat up in my seat and squinted out the window. "This Rohwer," Papa said. *Shii-chan* awoke, too, rubbing her eyes. Mama stared vacantly out the window. Soon, underwater-like murmurs filled our compartment. My ears were plugged from a cold.

I heard a man say, "Am I in a stupor or what? Is this Rohwer?" With a laugh, he said, "Looks like they've got us where they want us. Somewhere in the middle of nowhere."

"Look over there," someone else said. "That's our camp. . ."

Another man murmured, "Where's the cotton?"

A woman interrupted in Japanese, "I wish you'd stop joking we're lucky they didn't send us to Japan."

"Look out there," the man said, "Do you prefer this place to Japan?"

"Of course. We're in a war," she said.

"You're crazy. . ."

They bantered back and forth until the conductor said, "Everyone to the rear, folks."

Mama looked upset.

"How is your father doing?" Papa asked in Japanese.

"*Yokunai.* . . Bad; delirious," she answered. "They may have to operate." While they talked, I peered out the window again. Beyond the wire fence stretched row upon row of barracks.

Shii-chan peered out the window and asked, "Is this Rohwer?"

"Are you kidding?" I said. "Where have you been?"

"This place is for soldiers," she said.

Mama combed *Shii-chan's* hair and looked troubled. She kept looking back.

"What are they going to do with your father?" Papa asked.

"I don't know," she said. "His foot is so swollen, I'm afraid to look at it. The doctor told us they had to do something right away. The poison is spreading."

"It sounds very serious," Papa said, pulling our suitcases down from the overhead racks. "Your father will have to trust the doctor."

We climbed off the train to board trucks. Soldiers helped the women and children and a soldier helped me up too.

We sat with strangers on a bench. *Rok-san, Obasan,* and *Takashi* sat facing us. When the truck started, I peered into the cab. We were behind a line of olive green trucks, which turned at a sign that said "Military Police." At the gate, a soldier waved us on. Suddenly rain pelted our truck like hailstones. They sounded like bullets on the canvas, and I covered my head to block the barrage of sound. But when the exhaust fumes blew in, I pinched my nose. Everyone else covered their faces.

Two soldiers lowered a flag buffeted by the wind. They brought it down like a flapping fish. The white stars and red stripes reminded me of school and the Pledge of Allegiance. I could hear second bell, the one I often missed. Down an empty hallway, I would walk to the cloakroom. I could smell Harold's salami sandwiches in the brown paper bag. The lunch I wished I had. I could see Mrs. Henderson leading us in the pledge with her glasses propped on the bridge of her nose, blowing a note on a wee harmonica tied to a chain that went around her neck, "H-m-m-m-m-m, children, 'God,'" she said, stretching the word, "Again, 'God . . .'" She waited for us to join her. "Altogether now," she would finally say, "God bless America, land that I love . . ."

The barbs on the wire fence shimmered. Our truck whined. We bobbed forward and back, forward and back. Each jerk, each jolt, without a word. Which barrack will be ours? I wondered. We were somewhere in the middle of the center with barracks all around us. Here and there, activity. Men chopped wood, strung lines, and unloaded trucks. But the towers loomed. No question, we were prisoners. As we neared the edge of a forest, I heard the driver say,

"Block Eight," like a train conductor. Were we on a train? No, this was a truck.

"This Block Eight?" Papa asked, peering out through the canvas. The small wooden sign next to large building had the number eight painted on it. Everyone around me began to pick up belongings. Papa was the first one to climb out. He took the suitcases and bags, which *Rok-san* handed him.

The rain had stopped but the ground was wet. A bearded man, who had arrived weeks earlier, raked leaves near the truck. Small piles lay scattered in the open area. Near the ditch smoke rose from a metal drum.

"We in Barrack Two," Papa said to *Rok-san*, pointing at the barrack. The smoke in the air smelled good. It curled away in the breeze.

"We're in Three," *Rok-san* said. "No one will ever find us here," he added with a chuckle. We laughed, but it was true. But I also thought, they've taken us to a place where we won't be able to find our way back home, either.

Some nights I couldn't sleep. The wind came through the floor. Worse yet, everyone snored, even *Shii-chan*. I tossed and turned from one side to the other, unable to find a comfortable spot. I hated my bed. The mattress was thinner than a quilt. And to keep warm, I had to wrap the blankets around me. If I had to go to the bathroom, I was in trouble. Either I dressed, went outside, and walked a mile, or used Papa's *chamba,* or bedpan. I'd toss and turn, and wonder how long I could hold out. Without a clock in the room, I had no idea of time – I looked out the window for the morning light, but it was usually dark. I would drift in and out of sleep, and in my half-sleep, I would often wonder whether I was dreaming. Had I already gone? Yes I did, but it was in my dream. I still had to go. Darn. What should I do?

One night, I struggled until I couldn't hold out any longer. I climbed out of my cot and tip-toed to Papa's cot. Down on hands and knees, I found the handle and pulled. When I heard it splash, I stopped. Carefully, I pulled again, and gently and drew it out. I set its lid on the floor and positioned myself. But the smell was strong.

I hurried back to my cot and pulled on my pants. With a flashlight in hand, I tip-toed out the door. A full moon shone through the branches and lit the walkway. When I walked past the mess hall, I saw someone inside. The light was on. I smelled coffee and bacon. Mmm.

When I opened the door to the bathroom, warm air struck my face. A kettle of water steamed on the stove and the windows were frosted. *Uchida-san* sat near the center of the line of toilet bowls reading a book. He looked up and smiled. Mama said that he taught Japanese school before the War. While I peed in the trough, he said, "Sure gets cold here, doesn't it?"

"Yes," I replied politely.

"I like it better here than in my unit," he said. "It's quiet in here."

"I know what you mean," I said, "All that snoring keeps me up, too."

He laughed and said, "I can't leave the light on in my unit to read either." It didn't seem strange to talk to him while he sat on the toilet. But Mama and other women in the block complained about women conversing in the bathroom even though they had partitions. "Some women just don't care," Mama said.

When I returned to the barrack, I put the flashlight down, undressed and slipped into bed. It felt good to be warm and comfortable again. As I was about to sleep, I heard a clatter, then Papa's voice, "*Nan-ja*? What's this?" he said, and the light bulb over the table came on. I had to squint to see him. He sat in a chair, holding a foot in the air, while wiping it with a towel. I'd forgotten to cover the *chamba* and slide it back under his bed. I turned away before he saw me and pretended to sleep.

After that, Papa always made sure to place the *chamba* near the door before going to bed.

Chapter Fourteen

"Do you think he'll make it?" *Rok-san* asked. He and Papa were seated at the table when I walked in.

"I hope so," said Papa, "But he's lost a lot of blood."

"I shivered when I heard them sawing," *Rok-san* said. He looked at me and then at *Shii-chan* and then whispered to Papa, in Japanese, "It was worse when I heard the leg fall into the metal tub."

"I know," said Papa, "It was awful."

"Good thing he was asleep . . . Where is *Katsuye?*" *Rok-san* asked.

"Mama's in the bathroom," *Shii-chan* said, tossing a rubber ball in the air and scooping up jacks. "She said she'd be right back."

When Mama came in, *Rok-san* looked down at the floor and said, "I'm sorry about your father."

"Thank you," Mama said, in Japanese, with watery eyes.

"Your mother shouldn't blame you," Papa said to Mama, "You only told her what the doctor said."

"That doctor was dumb," *Rok-san* said. "They didn't even have hot water in the barrack. They should have had the decency to take him to a proper hospital."

"I know. . ." Mama said quietly. "But there was no time . . ."

"I'm sorry. I didn't mean it that way. I only meant that . . ."

"*Shikata ganai.* It can't be helped," Papa said to Mama. "It's not anyone's fault. There's nothing we can do about it now." Sometimes I wondered, though. If they had complained sooner, they may have given him the help he needed.

As it was, the poison had spread too far. *Ojii-san* died on a cot in the barrack, and *Obaa-san* bitterly mourned his death. She said his leg had been lost needlessly. "He was going to die anyway. Why didn't they let him keep his leg?" she said. *Ojii-san's* remains went to a crematorium and his ashes were delivered to *Obaa-san*. She kept the urn on the table with his picture. Whenever we went to see her, we prayed before the *butsudan* as we had before the war. But the prayers had deeper meaning now. I would place three pinches of granular incense into the smoldering urn, already filled to the brim with gray incense ashes. Her room always smelled like a funeral service. She never stopped praying. After we said our prayers, *Obaa-san* would brew tea and recall the events that led to *Ojii-san's* death. She would recall the loss of his leg, and say it was disgraceful to have to appear before Buddha that way. And then she would say in a venomous tone to Mama, "He could have kept his leg. Why wouldn't you listen?" Mama would listen quietly, but once we got outside, with misty eyes, she would tell me and *Shii-chan* not to worry about what *Obaa-san* said. "I didn't want to see my father lose his leg, but he wanted to live. He gave the doctor permission to remove his leg, but your grandmother won't believe me." And then came the question of his remains. Grandma did not want to bury him in the Rohwer cemetery. Rohwer was not the place that Grandpa would have chosen to remain. It was a remotely located parcel of land that the American government had chosen to jail the Japanese. And that was why Mama supposed, that Grandma insisted on keeping the urn with Grandpa's remains in her barrack apartment, just in case she should someday return to Stockton, when the War was over.

My sixth grade teacher, Miss Bramhall, said that Rohwer was reclaimed land. "Built over a swamp," she explained, "The army filled it with dirt. The ditches around every block empty out at the old swamp beyond the forest. There's precision to the construction. The army laid it out in lines and rows . . ."

The front of every barrack had doorways and porches and faced the front of another. The backs had no doors, but faced each other, too. In time they became back yards where children played, women hung laundry, and vegetables grew. Each block contained thirteen barracks, three pairs on either side of the mess hall. The extra barrack, the rec hall stood in the corner of our block near the forest.

Crawl spaces under the floors of the barracks were ready-made for hiding. Hide and seek was popular in our block until a boy, who always hid himself well, came out screaming.

"*Hebi ja*! Snake!" someone yelled.

"*I-i-yah . . . hebi*? *Hebi wa dai kirai*. I hate them," a lady said.

"Where . . . ?" the block manager asked the boy. "Where did you see it?"

"There . . ." the boy pointed. "It was really big." He held his hands wide apart.

A man with a rake said, "Here? You mean over here?" He banged the rake handle against the wall. Then turning it around, he stirred the dirt, and banged the boards with the handle again.

"*Oi, chotto-matte* -- wait a minute," a wiry white-haired man said. He motioned everyone back. Removing his hat, he peered under the barrack. Then with a long stick he poked around. He looked like a mechanic under a car. Finally, a snake as thick as a milk bottle came slithering out.

"Wow, that's a diamond back!" I heard someone say. "Look at the size of it." One man jumped when the snake twisted as the old man pinned its head to the ground. It continued to twist and writhe like salt water taffy. And then the old man stabbed it with a hunting knife. We followed him while he dragged it to the far end of the block to the chin-up bar. He stood on a box and tied the snake's head to the bar.

"What kind of a place is this?" Mama whispered with a tremor. "I'm afraid to go to the bathroom now."

Papa laughed. "They were here first," he told her in Japanese. "This was their home. I don't know what else lives in these woods, but we better be careful."

"Careful?" Mama said. "What do you mean, careful?" And Papa just laughed.

Papa and other men in our block went around pounding wash pans with sticks to flush out snakes, but were unsuccessful. Mama became vigilant -- she carried a flashlight and a club whenever she went to the bathroom after dark.

The snake hung from the bar with its rattles flat on the ground. I was afraid to touch it at first, but I did, anyway -- with my index finger. It looked wet and greasy, but felt dry. Its markings were like tapestry; I was repelled, yet attracted. How could a creature so beautiful be so dreadful?

The old man stood on a box. He held open the jaws and milked venom into a jar. When I asked him what the venom was for, he smiled. Through glinting gold teeth, he said, "Money, of course."

When he cut the skin away below its head, I thought of Papa's chickens. He gripped the skin with a pair of pliers and pulled down hard. My skin crawled with the ripping sound. It sounded like canvas, tearing.

When I returned later, the man was gone. What was left, hung tied to the bar, moist and raw. Without knowing why, I felt sorry for it.

One evening, Papa came home breathing hard. I suspected that something important had happened. " . . . for the whole camp," he whispered to Mama in Japanese, warming his hands on the stove. The kettle began to whistle, and Mama opened the lid on the can of tea and put three pinches into the pot.

"Whole camp what?" I whispered loudly. Papa thought I was asleep.

"Sh-h-h!" he whispered above the snoring from next door. "I tell you in the morning." Then to Mama he whispered proudly in Japanese, "I'm in charge . . ."

Papa had become the Director of Community Activities. He ran plays, talent shows, sumo and judo tournaments, movies, and other camp events. Though I'd felt proud, I was also bewildered. I didn't understand what his job meant. Was he working for the people who were keeping us in camp? Who was his boss? But Papa never talked about it, though most everyone knew. He, like everyone else, was working for the people who ran the camp.

The job was perfect. Papa liked being where he could be seen. "Good show tonight," he would tell me, "George Raft, Edward G. Robinson . . ." He knew the movies I liked. I'd hesitate at first, then decide to go at the last minute -- only to regret it later. You see, the film usually broke at a key moment, and the audience would shout its disapproval.

I would leave our barrack after I thought everyone in our block had left -- when I got to the field it would be near dark. I'd look for a place away from the projector, and avoid people I knew. A large part of the audience sat close together in a wide band between the projector and the screen; others sat in scattered groups. I'd sit behind the projector where the grass was thin.

When the sky grew dark, the light bulbs, which hung on sagging cords attached to skinny looking poles, would come on. Papa would make final adjustments, and the lights would go off. The screen would light up with images of a roaring lion, the searchlights of the 20th Century, or the Paramount mountains, and with them, I felt transported to a familiar world. Even films I'd already seen kept me riveted.

But it never failed. During a tense moment, Bogart's goodbye to Bergman, Lamont Cranston's transformation to Dr. Hyde, Stewart Granger swinging on a chandelier over a ballroom, the film would break, and then the screen -- in fact a bed sheet strung between goal posts -- would become white with light, as the sound would warble down. Within moments, the sheet was dark. People with flashlights played games with them. White spots chased white spots on the screen. But the booing and hissing would become louder until Papa turned on the light.

And there he was under a bucket of light in front of a microphone. The loudspeaker would screech while he cleared his voice. Rapping the microphone several times, bump, bump, bump, the screeching would get louder. When it finally stopped, he'd say, in Japanese, "*Mina-sama*, ladies and gentlemen, please excuse the short delay." And then he would ramble on about the quality of the film and how it had worn thin from overuse. People would begin to whisper, "Who wants to know? Who cares? Who is this bozo anyway?" More boos and hisses.

Papa would work furiously. Without seeing his face, I could see the beads of sweat on his forehead. But finally, the images would illuminate the screen, the projector would whir, and the lights would go off. With sporadic cheers and clapping we would pick up from where we left off. But within seconds, the film would break again.

More boos, but this time louder.

The images would fade from black and white to a disgusting yellow. For a brief moment the screen would light up, and then darken. I knew what had happened. The lamp in the projector had melted the film. I could smell the burnt celluloid in the air. By now people were standing and folding blankets.

"Please," Papa would say into the microphone, "Just a few more minutes."

After more complaining, a few spectators would sit down.

When "THE END" finally appeared and the lights came on, I would breathe a sigh of relief. But for Papa the evening had not been a disaster; he would smile and nod to everyone as if nothing had happened while the film rewound itself from front spool to rear spool.

It was hard to be the son of the Director of Community Activities. But even harder to understand why Papa kept on. Anyone else would have quit. But we had to be crazy then. How else can anyone explain our watching a Bogart film during the war on a bed sheet in the middle of nowhere? We were as crazy as the sailors who watched Lana Turner on a carrier in the Pacific.

Mess hall food was often a surprise. We ate powdered eggs, processed bacon, chipped beef on toast, meat loaf, hamburgers, sausages, potatoes, stew, rice, bread, everything with a variety of spices and seasonings. We ate the ration that soldiers ate, except that we didn't have a mess hall sergeant. Our cooks didn't go to culinary school. In time, we did not question the fare. We ate whatever they served us, mistakes and all. But I often yearned for Mama's cooking. I missed her tempura, teriyaki, nishime, sushi, steamed rice and picnic bentos. Most of all, I missed store-bought cookies, cakes, pies and Mama's jello. Her strawberry jello had always been one of my favorites. I loved to squish it around in my mouth until it melted down to a sweet liquid before I swallowed it.

One evening while waiting in line for dinner I was surprised to see it. There it was on a tray, unmistakable in its translucency. And strawberry... mmm, my favorite flavor. But as I drew nearer, it didn't look like what Mama used to make. Her jello always looked more broken and ripply. She would place small scoops of it into shallow bowls, and *Shii-chan* and I would eat it by the spoonfuls. This jello was smooth like meat and cut into cubes.

I picked up a cube of the stuff with metal tongs, and placed it on my plate between the corned beef hash and cabbage. I was afraid it would melt if I placed it too close to the rice.

After woofing down the hash, cabbage and rice, I went for the jello and jabbed my fork into it, but it resisted. I jabbed again, pushed even harder, but the tines didn't leave a mark. Pinning the cube down like I would meat, I tried cutting it with my butter knife, but it curled away like a rubber ball.

Lifting it off the plate, I dropped it and it bounced. I called to Ken and *Etsuo* who sat at the end of the table and showed them what I could do with jello. Soon other kids in the mess hall were throwing their dessert on the floor.

"Hey, look . . . look how high mine bounced. . ."

The adults, who had initially looked on with amusement, became annoyed. "Go play outside," they said. "Not in the mess hall!"

Some of us went back and scooped up leftover jello.

That evening we threw the cubes against the wall to see whose bounced back the farthest.

In all of the camps, the internees provided the labor. Rohwer was no exception. The *Hakujins*, who ran our camp, lived in separate buildings outside the fence. They worked for the WRA (War Relocation Authority). We only saw them when they made special announcements or distributed information. They never came to our block and ate in our mess hall nor did they participate in any of our events.

Ken *Oka* said we were slaves. "No one in his right mind works for sixteen dollars a month," he said. And that's what everyone was paid: cooks, janitors, dishwashers, truck drivers, typists, teachers, and hospital workers. Doctors were paid nineteen dollars a month, because doctors were special. Medicine was a highly regarded profession, so they received three dollars more a month than anyone else. "What a joke," said *Oka*. A few internees would argue that three dollars went a long way then -- a candy bar cost a nickel, and automobiles cost less than a thousand dollars. Papa's new car with radio, seat covers and floor mats cost six hundred dollars.

To Ken *Oka*, the problem was not money. He said that we were prisoners-of-war under the Geneva Convention. "They forced us to sell everything and put us in rooms without a stick of furniture," he said, angrily. "Why am I making cabinets and shelves out of scrap lumber? Why? I'm a prisoner of war."

"We have no choice," the block manager told him. "If we don't do things for ourselves, it won't get done."

"Don't you see?" Ken said, "They're not going to let us starve. Tell them to bring their own cooks, dishwashers, drivers, doctors and whoever and whatever. Make it their problem, not ours."

"That man is crazy," Papa said, "If he no careful, FBI take him to jail." And many of the *Issei* in our block agreed with Papa. Matters could be a whole lot worse. At least we had food and a roof over our heads.

But what Uncle Ken and his friends did shocked everyone, most of all, Papa.

"He did what?" Papa shouted in Japanese.

"I told you," Mama said. "He volunteered."

"Why? After what they did to us, why should he fight in their army? He may never come back."

"Don't say that!" Mama shrieked. She picked up the wash pan and I thought she would throw it. But she didn't. Instead, she put on a sweater and went outside.

Uncle Ken told Papa, "My friends and I are tired of being cooped up like this. We were born in this country. We are Americans."

"But look what they did to your father. It doesn't matter where you were born," Papa said in Japanese. "You look Japanese. That's all that matters in this country."

"My father didn't accept help when it was offered. I don't like being here anymore than anyone else, but I am an American. I am not Japanese."

"*Kichigai- ja*! You're crazy."

"But why should I sit idly by while my country is at war?"

"If you are an American, what are you doing in here?

"That question will be answered after the war is over."

"If you go, you are doing what they want you to do," said Papa.

"What they want us to do is not cause any trouble."

"How you cause trouble, if you join army?"

"We will prove them wrong. Isn't that the tale of *Chushingura*? Didn't the forty seven samurai slay *Kira* and prove their government wrong?"

"No, they kill *Kira*, then *hara-kiri*, so government no can kill them," Papa said in Japanese.

"No, that's not the way I understood it," said Uncle Ken. "When they killed *Kira*, they became heroes. The government did not know

94

how to punish them without bringing the wrath of the people on themselves."

Papa did not reply.

"The government did not know what to do. Finally, they asked the priests to intercede. The priests asked the warriors of *Asano*, the forty-seven samurai, to commit *seppuku* in order to save the government's face. When they did, they brought honor upon themselves and their master. They became folk heroes and proved the government wrong. At least, that's how I understood the story."

"How you know this?" Papa said, disbelievingly.

"My father told me," said Uncle Ken.

"*Soh . . .*" said Papa. "I still think you make big mistake."

Like Papa, I often wondered why my uncle would join the army to risk his life. He was more American than I ever could be. He did not ponder the color of his skin. And yet, I wondered. Maybe the meaning ran deeper. Maybe it was *bushido*. Maybe *gaman*, *shikkari* and *gambare* did have meanings for him as they did for me.

In early 1943 the WRA began registering adults in the internment centers for the purpose of releasing them, while the the War Department was also registering men for the draft. They both used a form entitled "Application for Leave Clearance."

Feelings about the internment in Rohwer had been divided. Many adult *Nisei* -- second generation Japanese Americans -- and *Kibei* -- those born in America, but educated in Japan -- were outspoken about their civil liberties. Most of those born in Japan -- or the *Issei* -- quietly accepted their fate.

Confusion led to disorder when the "Application for Leave Clearance" questionnaires came out. There were two questions, Question 27 and Question 28 which the internees thought unfair. The more outspoken among them asked: why are we, who are citizens of this country, who have been forcibly evicted from our homes and interned without cause being asked to serve in the armed forces?

Question 27: Are you willing to serve in the armed forces of the United States on combat duty wherever ordered?

Question 28: Will you swear unqualified allegiance to the United States from any and all attack by foreign or domestic forces, and foreswear any form of allegiance to the Japanese Emperor, or any other foreign government, power, or organization?

I heard Papa and *Rok-san* ponder these questions. "If we answer yes to 28," said Papa, "We lose our Japanese citizenship."

"I know . . . " *Rok-san* said, "but *Asaye* and I don't ever want return to Japan."

"Even if Japan were to win the war," Papa said, "I don't think I would go back either." I was surprised to hear him say this.

Papa and *Rok-san* met with others in the mess hall to discuss the questionnaire. "But *Omi-san*, do you understand the question?" *Shimamoto-san*, a *Kibei*, had asked.

"And what did you say," whispered Mama. She didn't want our neighbors next door to hear.

"I said, 'Of course I understand. Do you think I'm stupid?'"

"Lower your voice," Mama whispered, "Everyone will hear you."

"I don't care who hears me. I told them I am not a traitor. I love Japan. But I don't want to go back. I went back once before. I told them: I thought I left this country for good. But I came back. And then I asked them: you know why?"

Mama sat quietly in her chair. "If you say yes to both questions we will be without a country."

"You don't have to tell me that," he snapped. "You're beginning to sound like them."

"I agree with you," Mama said, "We wouldn't be happy in Japan."

Papa ignored her. "I told them that in 1922, after slaving in Petaluma for five years for money my father received, I went back to Japan. I was so happy to be returning home. I thought that I would be rich and my family would live in a big house. But then the big earthquake struck in 1924. We lost everything. Everything! So I came back to America to work so I could send more money home. I had so many brothers and sisters in Japan, and they had so many children. I kept them fed for a long while, but after I married in 1929, I said no more. I cannot continue this way forever. I have my own family to feed. And that is why I don't want to go back to Japan, I told them. 'You understand?' I said, 'That is why!'"

"And what did they say to that?" asked Mama.

"*Tamura-san*, an *Issei*, stood up and said to everyone in the mess hall, 'Listen to what he said. You youngsters don't know anything. It's one thing to wave a flag and another to feed a family.'"

"But when a *Kibei* from another block said, 'Shut up and sit down, troublemaker, or else you'll get hurt,' I said, '*Baka*! Sit down, you idiot Listen to your elders or get out of here!' The young man finally did sit down. These youngsters think they know everything. I told them how hard it was in Japan, but they didn't listen. They didn't believe me. They don't know what it is to starve in Japan."

Those who argued against the questionnaire were sent to Tule Lake. But during the meeting other questions had been asked: "Why must only we prove our loyalty? What about the Germans and Italians in America? Why haven't they been arrested?" According to Papa, someone in the room angrily replied: "Come on, Ken, why do you think we're here? Where have you been all your life? *Hakujins* stand up for *Hakujins*. After I graduated college I worked in my uncle's market carrying lettuce crates for three years. All my white classmates got jobs with companies like General Motors and Ford. Germans and Italians are white. We live in white America. That's why they put us in this stinking place. Anyway, what can we do about it, when they have the guns?"

Soon after that meeting, Uncle *Kazuo's* letter arrived from Tule Lake, *Rok-san* and *Obasan* said they had received a similar letter, and came to our unit to talk about it.

"Where's *Takashi*?" Mama asked, moving chairs to the table.

"He's sleeping," *Obasan* said. "Our neighbor's daughter is with him."

"That girl is *kanshin*. She's praiseworthy," Mama said. "She looks after her grandmother, too."

"I know . . ." said *Obasan*. "And she's only twelve. . ."

"Her father taught Japanese school."

"He did . . .?

Rok-san interrupted. He said to Papa in Japanese, "We came here to talk to you because our neighbors are nosy. But now I'm not sure who's nosier." And he laughed.

"Did you hear about the cook?" Papa said.

"Yes," replied *Rok-san*, "They beat him up. He had it coming anyway. He went around telling everyone to answer yes to the questionnaire."

"But now his family is mad. They want to get even. Everyone is crazy. And now we get this letter from *Kazuo*," Papa said. "He's returning to Japan and wants to take his boys with him."

"At least he's not asking for money," *Rok-san* said with a chuckle.

"*Soh*. . ." Papa said with a smile. "But why does he want to go back?"

"Maybe he feels an obligation," *Obasan* said.

"Obligation? To whom?" *Rok-san* said.

"It's different when you are the first-born son," *Obasan* said.

"*Kazuo* is *kanshin*," Mama said.

"*Kanshin*? He's not noble," Papa scoffed. "Not after all the money he took from us. *Rok-san* is right. If anything, he is stupid. He kept sending our money home and got nothing back. And why is he taking his boys with him? They can hardly speak Japanese. It's stupid. I never could understand him."

"But he makes a good point," *Rok-san* said. "His son Ben joined the army before the war."

"That has nothing to do with him or his family," Papa said. "Such things don't matter in this country. He should know that."

"What will his children do in Japan?" *Rok-san* said.

"*Kazuo* will regret this someday," Papa said, "But it will be too late."

In the end, *Kazuo* proved wrong. He and his sons never boarded a ship to Japan. Instead they remained in Tule Lake. And after the unconditional surrender, as a part of an amnesty, his boys, and others like them, regained their citizenship. But the memories of their actions were indelible. The *Nisei* who fought in Europe, who'd seen their comrades die, scorned No-No Boys like *Kazuo*; the people who had answered "No" to both Question 27 and Question 28.

The army veterans answered, "Yes –Yes" to the questionaire to prove to everyone that no matter their personal circumstances, their citizenship to the United States of America was deep founded and that they would give up their lives for the sake of defending their country from all enemies, domestic or foreign.

"They were cowards," the veterans said privately, of those who had answered no-no. "We risked our lives so that they could become citizens again." The No-No Boys became unspoken skeletons in the Japanese American closet.

Some forty years later, the No-No Boys were vindicated, hailed as heroes, applauded for the courage of their convictions. Yet, who today can remember the anguish when brothers, uncles and cousins, left the internment centers to become soldiers -- or the tears, when they didn't make it back, or the shock to see a brother or uncle return without a leg.

When the war ended, Uncle *Kazuo* became a recluse, a mere skeleton of the man who had once ruled the clan. His three sons and one daughter were married, and he had ten grandchildren. His children lived in the Bay Area, and were busy rebuilding their lives, while he lived in the basement of an apartment building and worked as a janitor. When he came to visit us, he would bring fish in a jar that he pickled himself. Though Papa loved to eat his fish, he did not appear grateful. His replies always seemed distant, above the steam and the roar of the pressing machine, whereas Mama was more courteous. She served him tea and crackers. And while Papa and Mama worked, I spoke to him.

"Do you have any girlfriends?" he would ask.

"No," I would reply, bashfully.

"You will, you will. Don't worry, you will. There's no need to hurry," he would say with a smile. "When I was your age, we didn't have washing machines and refrigerators. But look now. No one can do without them. Everything is changing. Don't forget the important things in your life. Make your parents proud."

After a short visit, he would smile, pick up his shopping bag and say he had to get back to his apartment. He would accept my offer to drive him home. While I drove, he kept saying how nice it was to live in San Francisco.

Papa could not forgive Uncle *Kazuo* while he lived. After a few drinks during dinner he would grouse about his early days in America and how he had been conscripted to an apple dryer in Sebastopol, a story we'd heard many times over, but one which in the telling, he never forgave his brother.

Years later, in 1952, Uncle *Kazuo* became ill with cancer, and Papa and *Rok-san* went to see him frequently. He was in his daughter's care in Berkeley. She said it warmed her heart to see them come to her home to see him. She said they never seemed like brothers while she grew up in Petaluma. But she said they came to see him almost every day while he was dying.

It was a sad day, indeed, when Papa and *Rok-san* wept openly before *Kazuo-san*'s casket.

Chapter Fifteen

From Block Eight, school was more than a mile away. *Shii-chan* walked with her friends, but I took my own path. I felt satisfied walking alone, doing whatever struck my fancy, cutting through other blocks, peering into mess halls windows, throwing stones into ditches, snapping twigs, stomping on leaves in the woods, and sprinting across the open field like a running back. On warm days, the air sang with grasshoppers. By cupping my ear, I could hear them beating their wings. I'd wait for one to land on the short grass, and then sneak up on it. I was careful not to let it see my shadow, and then I'd swiftly bring my hand down, and cup it. Then, I'd flatten my hand, gently, until I felt it. Keeping it pinned that way, I'd slowly uncover it and look for its thin toothpick-like legs. I'd pinch them together at the joint and bring the creature up close to my face. If it were really large, I'd feel like I'd won a prize. Then I'd throw it into the air, and watch it fly away and wipe off the brown stain on the grass. I'd catch a butterfly the same way: sneak up from behind while its wings were closed, then pinch its wings together. I'd wipe the powder off on my trousers. I enjoyed walking to school until I met David.

David lived on the other side of my block. I'd seen him at the mess hall, but didn't speak to him. I discovered later that he scowled even when he smiled. He usually ate with his older sister, Frances. She knew almost everyone in the block. Older boys tried to date her, but she always turned them down. After a while, they said she was stuck up. I thought she was nice. She reminded me of a girl I once secretly admired in the fifth grade. I couldn't talk to her without feeling guilty. She probably thought I was strange because I'd get nervous and stammer.

After school and on weekends, David would help his sister with laundry, hanging wet sheets and pillowcases on a clothes line. I'd hear him complaining, but she'd just tell him to grow up. No one else could talk to him that way, with the possible exception of his father. Mama said that his father was an ornery old man who once cooked in our mess hall. Mama said he quit the day after everyone got sick. She said the restroom was crowded with people the night of Thanksgiving. "They were all complaining about the turkeys," she said. "Mr. *Tamaki* didn't cook them long enough. They were too rare."

But Mama privately said it was Papa's fault. He wouldn't accept the blame. "*Tamaki* asked me how long the turkeys should stay in the oven, and I told him, 'Not too long, otherwise the meat will get too dry.' I didn't tell him to undercook them. Cooking that many turkeys in one afternoon isn't easy, particularly for someone who doesn't know how to cook," Papa said. I didn't know whether David had heard about the turkey episode from his father and whether it would have anything to do with the way he felt about me.

On my way to school one morning, while zig-zagging across the field, I heard David come up from behind me, "Slow down, man, slow down!" he said.

When I stopped at the edge of the grass, he scowled. A pinkish scar grooved his cheek. "Where you from, man?"

"San Francisco," I said, rather proudly.

"Frisco, huh? What's a turkey like you doin' in Rohwer?"

"My grandparents owned a hotel in Stockton," I said.

"Stockton, huh? Are you tough, or what?" He put his books down, rolled up his sleeve and flexed his biceps. "Punch me here, man," he said, pointing with a finger, "With everything you've got."

Suddenly I remembered the bully in the schoolyard in San Francisco, the kid who thought I was Chinese. This time I wouldn't back down.

We began our punches six inches from clenched fist to arm. Then, with each punch, the distance was increased to twelve inches, and then to eighteen. When he said, "Now, it's my turn," I tried not to wince.

His eyes widened. "Not bad man," he said, and then sneered, "Let's try one more."

That night when Mama saw the bruises on my arm, she asked, "What happened?"

"Football," I said.

"Maybe you shouldn't play that game anymore."

"I'll be all right," I said.

After that, David would wait for me in the woods. He was mad that I was ahead in school. We were supposed to be in the same grade, high sixth, but Rohwer didn't have half grades. They put him in the sixth, and me in the seventh grade. "It's all your fault," he would say, "If it wasn't for you, I'd be in the seventh grade."

"I don't know why they would do that," I said, "Why don't you ask the teacher?"

"Don't tell me what to do," he said.

"I'm just being helpful," I said.

"You're a wise ass," he said, and pushed me up against a tree.

During recess, David would bully me to show off. Once, he spun me around and threw me into a ditch.

"You'll be sorry," I had shouted, tearfully. "One of these days you'll get yours, you'll see! I'm gonna get even with you"

"Not by you, pipsqueak," he shouted and walked away laughing with his friends.

"Someday," I vowed, "Someday." I was never so angry in my life. The mud smelled rotten. I showered in Block 23 with my clothes on and wore the damp clothes home. After I soaked and washed them in the laundry, I hung them on the line. When Papa and Mama came home later, I didn't tell them what happened. It was the worst day of my life. I'd never felt such humiliation, nor such frustration. There was nothing I could do about him. And I would have to suffer through the humiliation every day on my way to school.

But I got even. David picked a fight with someone he should have left alone. Sixth grade was playing football against seventh grade, and it wasn't even close. David couldn't score all afternoon. After we scored four touchdowns, our team captain let me play. Compared to the players on my team I was small, but with good blocking, I ran for good yardage. David shouted something at me from across the field, but I didn't understand what he said. It didn't matter; I was having fun. When we scored our fifth touchdown, David was furious. On the ensuing kickoff return, Henry (our captain) met David head-on, and David bobbled, then fumbled the ball.

"Nice play!" I yelled, hopping up and down, where David could see me.

With a scowl, he pointed a finger at Henry, and said, "You tripped me!"

"I hit you head-on," Henry said. "Ask anyone."

"Bullshit. You stuck out your leg."

"Straight on," Henry said, "Straight on!"

"Bullshit," David said again, his face getting red, "You came around the side. You wanna fight?"

"Come on, forget it, man," Henry said. "Game's over. Go home."

"What's the matter? You afraid of me?"

"No," Henry said, calmly. "Don't start something you can't finish."

"Listen, asshole, I can finish you off any time."

"Just name the time and place."

"Over there, he said, pointing towards the woods, "After school tomorrow, man. You better be there!"

"Don't worry," Henry said, evenly, "I will."

That night after dinner, David boasted to the boys in our block. Pounding his fist into his hand, he crowed, "Like this, man, pow . . . right in the face."

We huddled in front of a small fire near the rec hall, rubbing our hands. The older boys laughed. I stared into the fire and wondered. The following day after school, when I walked to the woods with Henry, David sneered, and said to me. "You're next, traitor." And for a moment, I felt a twinge of guilt, but then I recalled what he'd done to me.

My heart sank when Henry took off his shirt. He looked thin. But he skipped and shadow boxed well and began to look formidable. "Whenever you're ready," he said to David. David drew in a breath and flexed his arms. Stepping forward, then backward, he punched at the air: first his left fist and then his right. "Yeah," he said, "I'm ready."

They walked toward each other, Henry standing erect, fists held high, David low to the ground, crouched, with fists held low. When David got close, Henry danced.

David growled. He didn't like the dancing, and raced forward. He smiled when he thought he had Henry trapped. But Henry feinted, sidestepped, kicked up dirt, and smiled back at David.

They continued this way until suddenly, Henry stopped. Instead of running, David moved forward slowly, checking Henry's every move.

Henry feigned right, moved left, and David hurtled by him. Then Henry turned, flicked his fist, jabbing David' nose once, twice, three times, four . . .

David hesitated. Wiping at his nose, he moved forward again. But this time with his forearms higher.

Henry skipped backward and stumbled, breaking his fall with an outstretched hand. When a boy near him tried to help, Henry shook his head. He lay on the ground face up for a moment, and stared at the sky. David stood and waited.

When Henry rose, David pulled his fist back and pushed it forward twice like a piston, the way he punched my arm, but missed. Henry had rolled one way and then the other.

Now Henry was on his feet. He jabbed, bobbed, danced, ducked, and peppered David' face with punches. For the first time, I felt the forest around us, the smell of its floor, the shadows, the stillness -- moldy leaves and twigs covered with fungus.

David's eyes were slits. Blood smeared his face and the smell mingled with the forest. I wanted them to stop, but the fight was over. David had lowered his arms, unwittingly, and Henry had unleashed a hook. And, that was it, David couldn't get up. He was finished, but he refused Henry's outstretched hand.

I was free! Now I could walk to school without thinking about David. But why did I feel sorry for him? When he wasn't in the mess hall that night, I worried. Why? He got what he deserved.

The next day on my way to school, I heard him behind me. "Wait up, " he said. And I thought, not again.

"What's your hurry, man?" he said.

"I don't want to be late for class. Where were you last night?" Why did I ask that? Why should I care?

"I caught hell from my sister," he said, "My father's sick . . ."

"Oh . . . ?

"Yeah . . ."

Several weeks later, his father died and he didn't come up from behind me anymore. And that summer, he and his sister left Block Eight without fanfare. I never learned where they went or whatever became of David.

Chapter Sixteen

Rohwer. In my reminiscences, soft, mushy, clay in spring, baked as hard as rock in summer, and in the fall, the same earth, overlain with leaves of rusted orange, turned soft and cold in the winter. People, tall, short, fat, skinny, light and tanned, spoke English and Japanese in broken phrases with varying inflections and dialects. We were a family. We learned who to listen to, who meant business, who to go to for favors, who was friendly, who was not -- often the harsh turned out nice and the gentle, connivers. We were as different as the spoken language. In the mess hall, laundry room, shower, dojo, commissary, talent shows, sumo matches, movies, school, we sat with each other, spoke, laughed, praised, argued, cajoled, scolded – one big family -- married men, women, single, young, elderly, *Issei, Nisei, Kibei*, boys, girls, mothers, and teen-agers, oblivious to the outside world, comfortable with each other.

But not always. On hot summer days while the idle read, played *shogi, go,* or *hana,* in their rooms, the weary sat in chairs, fanned their faces in front of noisy fans. My friends and I often played in the shower. We'd refill the deep wooden tub with cold water and leap into it. With loud screaming and yelling, eventually someone would tell us to stop. "That tub is not meant for playing in," an old man would yell. "You've wasted the hot water." Of course, that man helped build the tub. Even though it was in our shower, he and his friends said the tub was theirs.

Occasionally, someone would come to our defense. "Let the kids play," a self-appointed arbiter would say, "They're just having fun."

And this would create a division, a faction. Such factions were common in Rohwer, some were more obvious than others.

In our first year we came to know most everyone by name. We came to know each other's pettiness and habits. After the second year, we knew each other as well as the seasons. Winter meant snow and ice. We wore black pea coats, wool scarves, and earmuffs, which were bought at the commissary or ordered from the Montgomery Ward catalog. It was not uncommon to see everyone dressed alike. Even women wore pea coats.

Men and boys, old and young, would huddle around large metal drums in which a fire smoldered. With collars turned up, we stomped our feet, blew on our hands and held them over the drum to keep warm. Soon, our teeth would stop chattering. Most men smoked cigarettes. They would pull out a square of tissue from a pocket, gently roll the tissue into a U, shake tobacco into it from a sack, cinch the yellow string by pulling on it with their teeth, put away the sack, then carefully roll the tissue into a cylinder, and lick it along its length, paste it down, twist the ends tight, then while letting it dangle from their lips, strike a wooden match on the side of the metal drum, and light the twisted end while drawing in a breath. Sometimes, I'd listen to the elderly bachelors converse. They were entertaining to listen to with their dialect, even though I couldn't understand what they said.

Then came spring. Melting snow and ice left mud everywhere. We walked in *getas* (tall wooden clogs) to keep our feet clean, but ironically spent more time prying mud off from between the wooden cleats, than we would in cleaning our feet had we not worn the wooden clogs.

Burlap sacks were good for doormats, but we didn't have enough to keep up with the mud. After a while, we'd leave our shoes outside and on a warm day the mud became as much a part of the shoe as the leather.

In the summer, my friends and I walked around in bare feet. We often went to the ditch near the forest and sank our feet in the mud or played in the cool grass near the rec hall. We also enjoyed the cold cement floor in the laundry room. But bare feet had its consequences. Athlete's foot became so widespread that we had to bathe our feet in potassium permanganate before stepping into the shower.

I'd spent afternoons and evenings after school at New City Cleaners listening to the radio, but in Rohwer, I didn't miss Captain Midnight, the Ovaltine commercials, or my decoder ring. Jack Armstrong, the Green Hornet, the Shadow, and the Lone Ranger had no place in Block Eight.

Summer days ran together. Had it not been for church (which we didn't attend), I would have forgotten Sunday. Football and basketball were popular in our block. I played with my friends in the open space behind the laundry room. Sometimes, we lifted weights. I learned how to "clean and jerk," "snatch," and "press." The techniques I learned well, but I couldn't "press" my weight no matter how hard I tried. On warm days, I would play marbles under a tree with boys younger than me.

I also took Judo lessons in the summer. The *sensei* gave out judo *gi* with belt rankings which went from white to green to purple to brown and black. I wore green. The boys who wore purple were too strong. They threw me to the mat before I could even set my feet.

Sometimes, I brought books home from the library. I enjoyed reading Zane Grey, Jack London, and Mark Twain. I shared their stories with a boy in my block. Soon, he brought books home, too, and shared them with me.

During the summer, I fished for crayfish in the ditch near the woods. I would punch holes in the bottom of an empty tomato can and tie strings to it. Then, I would put a piece of meat or bread inside the can and lower it into the water. Within minutes, I'd have a half dozen crayfish to play with. I liked the way they moved backwards with their claws held high.

I was the only boy in my block who played with snakes. I'd catch them the way *Tamura-san* did: by pinning them down with a forked stick and picking them up behind the head. Once, I stuffed a small snake into my pocket and took it to school. My classmates shunned me. My teacher made me promise never to bring a snake to class again. Despite my inner discomfort, snakes intrigued me.

I was at the age of testing. One day, I spent an afternoon with two high school boys near a stream outside Rohwer knowing that if we were caught we would be in trouble. These boys had found a hole in the fence and had kept it to themselves. And even though by the end of the first year, the soldiers knew about it, they only guarded it loosely, and it was still there. Still, everyone was warned to stay clear of it. A man in the Poston internment center had been shot just for wandering close to the fence.

I overheard the two boys talking about the stream one evening after dinner. They were lifting weights behind the laundry room. *Tak* had just "clean and jerked" 150 pounds, and was talking to *Yuki*. I thought I misunderstood when I heard *Yuki* say they went outside. "What do you mean outside?" I asked.

"Like I said, 'outside,'" *Yuki* replied flatly.

"Its your turn . . ." *Tak* said to *Yuki*.

Yuki sat down. "Nah . . . its too hot." He eyed me, and said to *Tak*, "This kid doesn't know what outside means," and laughed.

"Got any money?" *Tak* asked.

"Who me?"

"Yeah, you."

"Not much," I said.

"How much you got?" asked *Yuki*.

"About 45 cents," I said, fingering the coins in my pocket. It was money that *Obaa-san* had given me. She was always giving *Shii-chan* and me money wrapped in orange paper.

"That's enough for candy in McGehee," said *Tak*. "You want to go? We'll pay you after we get back."

"It's really nice out there," *Yuki* said, "There's even a stream about a mile from the fence." The thought of *outside* made me tingle. I lay awake in bed that night staring at the ceiling.

We left after lunch. "Behind Block Seven," *Tak* had said. Block Seven was deserted, except for the kitchen crew peeling potatoes. We jumped across a ditch and waded through thistle to get to the fence, which ran parallel to the ditch in both directions. Rain had washed away the dirt from around the post where wires had been cut. By now, I wasn't sure I wanted to go. The barbs looked sharp and my arms itched. I told *Tak* that I felt ticks under my arms. "Let me see," he said, pulling up a sleeve. He looked hard and pushed me away. "Nah," he said, "It's your imagination. There's nothing there."

"You sure?" I said.

"I wouldn't lie. Come on, let's go before someone spots us."

Tak made it look easy. He went through and held the wires apart He motioned *Yuki* through and then me. I looked to see whether anyone else might be around. "Hurry up," he said, "I can't hold it all day."

When my pants got caught, I panicked. Instead of taking my time to undo it, I tugged, until I heard it tear. Finally, I pulled free. My leg bled, but it didn't hurt. When *Tak* saw the blood, he looked worried. "Wait a minute," he said.

"I'm okay . . ." I said, examining my leg. "I'm okay," I said again with a smile.

"If you say so," he said, and hoisted me up.

Yuki stood in the tall grass. "Hurry up, you guys," he said.

The grass came to my chest. Its tips rippled like silk across the field. I ran behind *Yuki*. *Tak* was far ahead. He only stopped when he seemed to lose his way. When *Yuki* and I caught up to him, he would take off again in another direction, and we would have to run even faster to keep up. Soon, we were in a forest and the air smelled earthy, like Mama's *gobo*, or burdock._Our feet sank slightly in the leaves and twigs. How much farther? I wondered, when at last I saw *Tak*: he was on a wooden bridge, gazing over the rail. He laughed when he saw us breathing hard. "You guys are really out of shape," he said, picking up a handful of acorns and throwing them in the air. They soared like grasshoppers and made tiny splashes in the water. I, too, grabbed a handful of acorns and tossed them into the air. "Wow, this is fun," I said.

Tak pulled off his shoes, and rolled up his pants. "Come on," he said, "The water looks cool."

As we descended the embankment, I heard a man's voice from above. I stopped and froze like a stone.

"Careful boys," he said, "Water's deep, down yonder."

We're trapped, I thought. What now? Shifting my weight I felt the spongy earth underfoot. With the sun behind the man, I had to squint to see him. He was tall.

But he looked puzzled. Staring wide-eyed, he said, "How'd you boys manage to get out here?" He held a fishing pole in one hand and a string tied to a can in the other.

"Through a hole in the fence," *Tak* said, with a smile.

The man laughed, satisfied with *Tak's* reply. "You gotta be careful around these parts, boys. The bank is slippery, and the water runs fast and deep in places." He walked farther upstream along the embankment and found a flat area near the water. Placing his can on a tree-sized log, he tied fishing line to the end of his pole and baited his hook with a worm. Extending his pole over the water, he let his line swing back and forth and then flung his worm out to a point near a fallen tree on the far side of the pool. We watched him catch three catfish this way. Finally *Tak* said that we had to leave. "It'll be dark pretty soon," he said. "We'll have to save McGehee for another time."

We said our goodbyes to the man, and he said, "Nice to meet you fellas. Good luck."

Getting back wasn't easy. We ran in circles in the woods. "Hey," said *Yuki*, "We came back to the same spot. Look over there where the tree is fallen over. Don't you know the way back?"

"It's not easy," *Tak* said angrily. "You want to lead?"

"Nah," *Yuki* said. "Just don't keep coming back here."

Yuki kept complaining, and *Tak* would tell him to shut up. But anger turned to fear, when the forest kept getting darker. But finally, *Tak* did find the grass and then the fence.

When we got back to our block the security lights around the mess hall were on. I was hungry, but the mess hall was empty and dark. That hadn't mattered as much as not having made it to McGehee. I had sorely wanted to see the inside of a store again.

When, during our second year in Rohwer, Papa said that Japan was losing the war, I wondered how, after such an overwhelming victory in Pearl Harbor, that could be true. Besides, he often said that Japan had never lost a war. But now, he said that Japan was foolish for having started it. "America is too big," he said in Japanese. "Big mistake. America too far away." What ever happened to *Yamato damashi*? I couldn't ask this question without hurting him. From the very beginning with the attack on Pearl Harbor, I hadn't wanted Japan to win the war, but now I felt betrayed.

Many people had left Rohwer by then. *Nisei* had been allowed to leave for cities on the East Coast and in the Midwest. I had wanted to leave too. The waiting became harder when my friends started to leave. *Tak* and *Yuki* had gone with their families to Seabrook Farms, New Jersey.

"How long are we going to stay here?" I asked Papa.

"Too much danger outside," Papa said. "Too much *haiseki*. Prejudice."

I was surprised to learn that many families had gone from the Stockton Assembly Center to beet fields in Idaho. We could have gone too. In fact, we could have gone anywhere then, except California, Oregon and Washington.

In December 1944, the War Relocation Authority announced the closing of Rohwer. Many internees, including *Rok-san* and *Obasan*, did not want to leave. Japan was losing the war, and the America outside Rohwer seemed hostile. America's geography was frightening. Cities like Chicago, St. Louis, Detroit and New Jersey were foreign. Until the war was over, the internment center seemed like the safest place to be.

And that was the way Papa had felt. But as increasing numbers of people left Rohwer, his job became increasingly difficult. He began to sense the hopelessness of his work. With a dwindling cast of performers and assistants, his shows had become harder to produce. When complaints from the audience became more than he could bear, he decided to leave. He said to Mama one evening, "We wasting time here. I no like Rohwer. More money outside."

I'd heard him talk this way before so I wasn't prepared for what he said next.

"We go Denver."

"Denver?" I nearly fell off the cot.

"Denver good. High mountains. Good air. *Harada-san* say very good," Papa said enthusiastically. "He say Denver good to Japanese. Lots of work."

"Who's *Harada-san*?"

"You know . . . he always help me do talent show."

"Oh," I said, ". . . him. " The *Kibei*. The thin, anemic tenor who often sang in Papa's talent shows. Papa had enjoyed his singing. "*Harada-san*," Papa would say, "if you go Major Bowes Amateur Hour, you be *itoh sho*. First place," After that, *Harada-san* couldn't do enough for Papa. But when he left Rohwer, Papa lost his best helper. *Harada-san* often wrote from Denver and Papa would read his letters aloud. "I am sharing an apartment with a *Nisei* who grew up here . . ."

I was astonished. "You mean they didn't put Denver Japanese into camps?" I said.

"*Soh yo*," Papa said. "*Hakujin* only scare in California. Colorado too far from Japan." No matter what Papa said, I still thought it odd.

"There are many Japanese families in Denver," Tom wrote. "Should I find a nice apartment for you?"

Mama seemed relieved. She didn't want to be among the last to leave Rohwer. "It's good that we're leaving in the summer with school out," she said.

"Do we have to?" *Shii-chan* whined. She was playing solitaire on the floor.

"How far is it to Denver?" I asked with trepidation. Now that the decision had been made, I felt uncertain.

"I now know how long take," Papa said.

"How about *Rok-san* and *Obasan*?" I avoided mentioning *Obaa-san* for Mama's sake.

"I think *Rok-san* no want to go," Papa said to me.

The following afternoon I overheard Papa and *Rok-san* talking in Japanese. "It's crazy to stay here," Papa said. "Everyone's leaving. Look at how empty this place is getting. It's going to be hot again this summer, and the mosquitoes will be worse than last year. There won't be anyone left to do anything about it. *Fuji-san* says that we're already short on help in the mess hall. We should leave now, before matters get worse. Jobs in Denver pay much more than what they pay us here."

"But we feel safer here," *Rok-san* said impatiently. I'd never heard him raise his voice before, especially to Papa. "We wouldn't know what to do in Denver. I'd have to work while *Asaye* stays home. And what about *Takashi*? He's gotten used to everything here, even the mosquitoes."

"*Minoru* and *Shii-chan* could look after *Takashi* in Denver," Papa said.

"No, no, too much trouble. We'll stay here until they kick us out," *Rok-san* said firmly.

"All right, then . . . " said Papa, wiping his forehead, "I'll write you from Denver. But let me know if you change your mind."

No one said anything about *Obaa-san*. It was as if she didn't exist. *What will she do?* I wondered. Mama didn't seem to care.

Denver was a calculated risk. Papa gambled on a friend to help us, but how reliable was he? With mixed feelings, I looked forward to the trip as I would to an adventure, but wondered about the white population. Would boys taunt me in school? Call me Jap? Rohwer was emptying fast, though. We couldn't stay in here forever. Denver could provide a way of getting back to California someday.

Shortly after Papa decided on Denver, he began to have second thoughts. "Should we go to San Francisco instead?" he asked Mama one night. My heart skipped a beat.

"No," Mama replied, "*Osoroshi*. I'm afraid. *Okamoto-san* at the Director's office said there were shootings in Fresno, and a barn was burned down in Placer County. I think we should wait."

"But, Mama . . . San Francisco . . ." I whined.

"I heard about that too," Papa said.

And then he decided, "If we no like Denver, we go California."

A few days after the farewell party in the mess hall, Mama packed our suitcases and Papa wrote thank you notes to relatives and friends in camp. And then he placed fresh bills into envelopes, licked the tabs, and smoothed them down.

"Where did this money come from?" I asked in wonderment, as he placed the envelopes into money belts.

"I save," Papa said proudly.

"How much?" I asked.

"Shhh," Mama said. "They can hear you."

"How much?" I whispered.

"Six hundred," Papa whispered with a smile. "I save from before."

"Six hundred? Wow!"

"S-h-h-h-h-h," they both said.

Mama fastened my money belt under my shirt. I felt better about leaving now since we had money, but I had no idea of its worth. I wondered how long it would last. I also wondered about Tom *Harada*. Was he reliable? Could he help Mama and Papa find work?

As if he were reading my mind, Papa said, "*Harada-san* find good apartment, I send him deposit. He say, 'Owner Japanese, very good family, take good care of Japanese,' and he say, 'No worry about working. Cleaning business good in Denver. They paying one dollar to one dollar fifty cents hour, if I know how to do pressing.'" Papa laughed and patted my head.

I was sad to leave my friends. I didn't know whether I'd ever see them again. I was even sadder to leave *Rok-san*, *Obasan*, and *Takashi*. It was our first good-bye. And my poor grandmother. Papa and Mama had asked her to join us, but she steadfastly refused. "I have to go to Stockton," she said in Japanese. "I have to go to the hotel and find my things." *Rok-san* and *Obasan* promised Mama that they would help my grandmother when it came time for her to leave Rohwer.

After we boarded the train, I could see *Rok-san, Obasan,* and *Takashi* through the window. They stood behind the fence, with *Takashi* perched on *Rok-san's* shoulders. *Rok-san* took *Takashi's* hand in his and waved it and *Takashi* laughed, gleefully. The sadness of that moment touched me. We didn't know when we would see each other again. *Obasan* smiled through tears and waved with a handkerchief.

"See you in California . . . " I shouted, but they couldn't hear me. I waved, and so did Papa with a smile. Mama and *Shii-chan* waved from the seats opposite ours and I heard *Shii-chan* say goodbye several times. When the train jerked into motion, we stopped waving, then waved uncertainly when it moved forward again. I continued to wave, until I couldn't see them anymore. And suddenly, Rohwer with its paper barracks, mess hall, laundry room, snakes, crayfish, chiggers and wire fencing had vanished. Had I dreamed it? No. I still had the mimeographed copy of *The Rohwer Outpost* in my lap, with L'il Daniel in his coonskin cap on the cover.

The train moved steadily ahead. People moved about in the aisles, returned to their seats, while the compartment swayed. Papa stared vacantly out the window. We moved through a forest into a valley dotted with shed-like houses. In the distance I could see a dark silhouette of mountains against a cloud-streaked sky. As we got closer to the mountains, the trees became larger and the sky disappeared.

"Will we ever see them again?" *Shii-chan* asked Mama. She was staring out the window too. "Maybe after the war," she answered. Soon the train moved rapidly. It rocked from side to side and with this motion, my mind wandered, I imagined stores and shops, a bakery, a restaurant, a soda fountain and racks filled with comic books. The sun streamed in at an angle, and Mama lowered the window shade, but only slightly. I closed my eyes and heard a dog, barking, sirens, screaming, church bells, ringing . . . The locomotive whistle blew, and suddenly its smoke covered the mountains. Up, up, the train was climbing. Below us, a canyon, a riverbed; the train was turning, pulling a line of cars along a ledge, through a tunnel, and suddenly the compartment was dark, but only for a short while. The sun shone through again, but this time, across the aisle, on a man who slept with a newspaper over his face. Papa stretched his arms and yawned as the train ground on.

Chapter Seventeen

When we got off at the station, I searched for a friendly face. Oddly, I felt comfortable. We were in a small town outside Denver. The people were mostly *Hakujin* with a few black porters. Though we'd never been to this place before, it was in a familiar world. We'd come back. Yet, I also felt uneasy. We were like convicts who had come out of jail. Three years in prison and we were now free. But we hadn't been convicted of a crime; only of skin color, which we couldn't free ourselves from. Like convicts who wore striped uniforms in jail, we wore our skins outside.

We walked across a tiled floor and followed strangers through turnstiles toward exit doors. I carried a bundle in one hand and shaded my eyes with the other. Bright sunlight came through the windows. *Shii-chan* complained while holding Mama's hand. "That light is hurting my eyes," she said. Papa looked this way and that. As we got near the exit door, I touched the money belt under my shirt and felt gratified. It's still there, I thought.

"*Omi-san, Omi-san*," a man shouted. I recognized his voice, but could only make out his shadow against the light. People in the station turned to look. *Why is he shouting in Japanese?* I thought. Papa was no better. "*Harada-san*," he shouted back. "*Yoku kitekureta naa* -- thanks for coming." After the formalities of bowing and Japanese pleasantries, *Harada-san* took one of Papa's suitcases. "Let me help you," he said. "The car is out front."

When we stepped outside, a breeze cooled my face. It had been warm in the station. The sky was without a cloud and as blue as jeans. The sun shone bright. It felt good to be off the train and getting on a car.

"How nice the weather is," Mama said in Japanese, from the back seat. She sat with *Shii-chan* and Papa and I sat in front.

"It's been like this for weeks," he said, in Japanese. "Denver is not humid like Rohwer."

"*Soh*," Papa said. "I no like Rohwer."

"Denver is a mile high," I said. "The air is thinner here."

"*Soh*..." said *Harada*.

"But I like it better here," I said. "It's cooler."

"You have very nice car," Papa said in English. "Before War I have 1940 Dodge, but I like Chevrolet. Body by Fischer. I like shifting in steering wheel."

"I don't know about cars, *Omi-san*," he said in Japanese. "This one belongs to my roommate."

"Is your roommate Japanese?" I asked.

"Yes..." said *Harada*. "But he was born in America."

"Then he's *Nisei*," I said.

"He's just like we are, George..." said Shii-chan.

"Yeah, I know," I said. "But I wasn't asking you."

"It's nice to have a car," Mama said in Japanese.

"*Hai, Obasan*," *Harada* said, "Today is my day off. After I drop you off I have to pick my roommate up at work."

We were on a highway. I recognized the grills coming toward us by model and make, but I didn't mention them. I was more fascinated to be in a car again.

"Can I turn on the radio?" I asked.

"Yes, of course," *Harada* said, looking over his shoulder to change lanes.

"This car have good pick up..." Papa said, and then to me, he said, "Radio too loud."

I turned the volume down, just as the strains of "Besame Mucho" came on.

"*U-u-wah*," Papa said. "He sing just like you, *Harada-san*." I turned the volume up a notch.

Through the rear view mirror I could see *Harada-san* beaming, and for a brief moment we were back in Block Eight at the talent show.

"We're here," *Harada-san* said. He parked in front of a store with a show window, like the one in front of our cleaners on Polk Street. Tall letters in red, framed in gold leaf, painted on the glass, said, "Yamada TOFU," but the sign on the door read, "Closed." A man in a white apron, with his back to the door mopped the floor. The wet sidewalk smelled like vinegar.

A voice from above, shrilled, "*Harada-san* . . . Is that *Omi-san* with you?" We looked up to see a gray-haired woman with her hair in curlers. She poked her head out the window.

"*Hai*," *Harada* answered, "*Chodo ima tsukimashita* -- they just arrived." He handed suitcases to Papa and me and then went to the front of the car and pulled out a sheaf of papers from the glove compartment.

"One minute please," she shouted again. "I can't come down. I have something on the stove. My son is coming down."

"Thank you, *Sakamoto-san*," said *Harada*, "We will wait . . ." He handed Papa the mimeographed papers, and said, "I picked these up at the Japanese American Citizens League office. There's a map and other important things in here." He turned to face the stores, and said, "What I like about this place is that everything is close by. The grocery store," he pointed, "Is next to the barbershop, and the drugstore is over there." The block was lined with shops with apartments over the stores. *Harada-san* explained that this was an older part of town. Many buildings across the wide street looked dilapidated. Their front yards were weed-filled and their windows, boarded up.

The buildings on our street didn't look any better. The stucco above the tofu store was chipped and cracked and in need of paint. Further down the block, a large portion of the exterior wall was damaged. Chicken wire and tarpaper beneath the stucco were showing through. *Harada* was about to tell us more when we heard footsteps coming down the stairs inside the building. A man with short hair peered out the door. "Please come in," he said, with a toothy smile.

Harada smiled and said, "This is *Omi-san* and his family . . ."

Papa lowered his head and said, "*Hajime mashite*. Pleased to meet you . . .

The man also bowed and smiled, but appeared embarrassed. He paused and said, in English, "Nice to meet you folks."

Then *Harada* looked at his watch and said to Papa, in Japanese, "Excuse me, I cannot stay any longer. I have to pick up my friend at work. I am sorry to leave you this way, but I didn't know it was this late. Please call me at this number if you need me." He handed Papa a card.

"Thank you for your help today," Papa said, in Japanese. "I know you are busy, but we need your help in finding work."

"Yes, *Omi-san*. I know. Please look in the newspaper. I will also talk to my friends and let you know if I hear of anything. I will call you this evening."

"Thank you, thank you," Papa said, shaking his hand. *Harada-san* smiled, nodded, and turned to leave, but Papa didn't seem to want to let go of his hand. Finally, he did. With a hesitant bow, Harada-san walked to his car.

"You have telephone?" Papa turned and asked the landlady's son.

"Yes . . . In the hallway."

"He have this telephone number?" Papa asked.

"I'm sure he does . . . If not, he can always call my mother."

The landlady's son stood a head taller than Papa. While leading us up the stairs, he turned and said, "You folks are from Rohwer, aren't you?" His long narrow eyes became wide slits when he smiled.

"Yes, we just get off train. You know Rohwer?" Papa asked.

"No," he said, "I was born here."

"Oh. . . You live here all you life, Mr. *Sakamoto*?"

"Yes, *Omi-san*. My name is Kenneth. Please call me Ken."

Ken led us down a narrow hallway to our room. After he opened the door, he said, apologetically, "Not much furniture . . . Only the bare necessities. Our tenants are mostly Japanese and they usually fill in to suit themselves. It cuts down on storage. Of course, we pass these savings on to you." He handed Papa the key.

"What I smell?" Papa said, sniffing the air.

"The bucket under the sink," Ken said. "H-m-m . . . It does smell rancid doesn't it? I'll have to show you where to empty it, but, first, let me show you the rest of the unit." He took us into two bedrooms: one with a double bed, and the other with two single beds. Blankets, sheets, and pillowcases were stacked on the mattresses.

"Did *Harada-san* pay deposit?" Papa asked. "You know?"

"You'll have to talk to my mother. She makes all the arrangements. I'm only here for the summer. Oh. . . and by the way,

Mr. *Omi*, the bathroom is down the hall. It's shared, but as I said, everyone here is Japanese."

Mama ran her hand over the faded tile on the kitchen counter. She unwrapped a bar of soap and placed it in the dish. Papa struggled with the doors under the sink, but they wouldn't open.

"I guess the painters sealed them shut . . . " Ken said. "The kitchen water drains into a bucket under there . . ."

"You no have plumbing?" Papa said, with a scowl.

"No. Not for the drain. It's something we mean to add someday."

"You have screwdriver?" Papa said.

"Yes . . . sure, I'll get one for you."

I wondered why *Harada-san* hadn't mentioned the problem with plumbing in his letters and why he wasn't better prepared to help Papa and Mama find jobs. What we learned later from Mrs. Sakamoto was that *Harada-san* had been ill until recently. He'd been in a hospital for a month.

After Ken left, Papa grumbled to Mama in Japanese, "I never heard of such a thing. Even in Petaluma we had plumbing."

Mama nodded agreement, and smiled. "At least we can't hear our neighbors next door." And Papa had to agree that this apartment was better than the barrack we had in Rohwer.

Shii-chan and I went outside to take a look. "Isn't this fun to be in a city again?" I said, looking into the tofu store.

"No, I hate our apartment, that ugly bathroom. Everything smells."

"But the bathroom has plumbing . . . Doesn't it?" I asked. I wasn't sure.

"Yes, but it still smells."

The following night *Shii-chan* and I went for a walk again, but this time further down the street. We turned the corner and walked down a narrow street. "This place is spooky," *Shii-chan* said. "Let's go back. I'm getting cold."

"Let's just go around the block . . . We'll be back before you know it," I said. But the street was dark with only light from the moon coming down through the trees. As we walked farther down the block, I heard a clanging sound from across the street.

"What was that?" *Shii-chan* whispered.

"I don't know," I said. In the dim light I saw several boys throwing objects into an empty lot. "Come on," I said, "Let's go back."

"Hey, you . . ." one of the boys hollered, "Got any money?"

"Hurry up," I said, taking *Shii-chan's* hand.

"No," I yelled back.

"Hold it there . . ." he hollered. "I wanna talk to you." He and his two friends trotted across the street.

But when they got near the tree in the sidewalk, another voice from down the street, shouted, "Hey, man, what did I tell you the last time?"

The boy, nearest the tree, said, "We don't want no trouble from you, man. . ."

"Then, get out of here. I'm not telling you again. . ."

"Yeah, man."

The boy and his friends left -- the boy who shouted them away was a tall stout Asian boy. "They're harmless," he said. "Don't let them give you a bad time. If you see them again, let me know. I know where they live."

"Thanks . . ." I said.

"No sweat, man. Where you from?"

"Rohwer."

"Rohwer? You live around here?"

"Yeah. Around the block."

"The Sakamoto place?"

"Yeah . . . "

"That place is a fire trap."

The following week, Papa and Mama found work at a dry cleaning plant. Papa got along with the supervisor but didn't like the owner. "Mr. Diego, he like me," Papa would boast after work. "He teach me how to do spotting (\You know, removing spots off of garments. Now, I do myself. I no need his help." And I'd felt happy that Papa and Mama were working.

While Papa spotted, Mama pressed. Mama said that the owner kept them apart, because Papa slowed her down. He criticized her often. Even at home, he would tell her to be more thoughtful about pressing garments. "It's not piece work," he would say, "Especially, pants. If you're not careful, you will have double pleats." Mama knew that if Papa continued this way they'd both be in trouble, but she didn't argue.

Papa eventually quit his job, and so did Mama. "The owner thought Papa was too slow," she told *Shii-chan* and me privately, "Papa's too fussy. The owner got mad when he saw Papa brushing lint off a jacket I just pressed. When the other workers laughed, Papa told them to shut up. Then, the owner told Papa to mind his own business, but Papa wouldn't listen. He tried to show the owner the lint on the jacket. When everyone laughed again, Papa threw the jacket on the floor and told the owner he quit." Mama said he went to the time card machine, punched his card, and left. Mama quit too. But she said she hated looking for work. She had to find a job for Papa too. *Harada-san* wasn't much help in finding jobs for them.

Papa surprised us all one day. He came home in a car. "Look outside," he said, proudly, "1934 Oldsmobile, four door sedan. I only pay one hundred fifty dollars. It run good and very clean inside. Come outside, I show you," and he took us for a drive. I thought that we were off to a good start with our lives in Denver.

But to Papa's consternation, the engine had a cracked block that leaked, leaving a puddle of water under the car. During Sunday drives to a lake outside Denver, he would watch the needle on the temperature gauge rise. When it was about to inch into the red zone, he would pull off the road, wait for the engine to cool, and fill the radiator with water.

When he complained about this to Ping, the mechanic who sold him the car, Ping only replied, "This is Denver, Mr. *Omi*. Everything here freezes in the winter. You know that when water turns to ice, it expands. That's why cars in Denver have cracked engine blocks. I can replace yours at cost, Mr. *Omi*. One hundred dollars. I won't make a penny." What a crook, I thought. Papa should get his money back.

"No, I keep like is, Mr. Ping, but why you no tell me before?"

"I sold it to you cheap, Mr. *Omi*, but you can have your money back, if you like." Yes, yes, give it back, I thought.

"No, I keep," Papa told him. But whenever the car overheated, Papa would complain about how he had been outsmarted. "Chinese too smart," he would say.

My high school was several blocks from where we lived. I recognized a few boys during recess, but they weren't in any of my classes. I had been worried about the internment and living among *Hakujins* again. But oddly, I felt comfortable in this school. The student body was mainly black and Latino. My classmates said that most of the white kids in Denver went to high schools in the more affluent neighborhoods. It felt strange to be among blacks and Latinos, but I enjoyed watching them dance to recorded music. They danced to Duke Ellington, Lionel Hampton, Count Basie, Fats Waller and others. With school books tucked under my arms, I would tap my feet to the rhythms. The dancers jitter-bugged and swayed in an off-beat way. When I got home, I would try to move the way they did in front of Mama's full-length mirror.

I found it easy to talk to the Asian girls in school. We compared answers in math and notes on reading assignments. My outward interest in girls did not go beyond academics, though I often wondered what I had to do or say to make myself attractive to them. I envied boys with girlfriends.

Sometimes I'd play catch or basketball with boys in my neighborhood. I didn't know where they lived and had never been to their homes, but I found them easily. They were always in the street. A few of them worked in the bowling alley. And soon, I was working there in the evenings and on weekends, too. Whatever I earned, I gave to Papa. I wanted to help our family. I was also glad that Papa was pleased. He would place the money in an envelope and tuck it under the mattress. "You big help now," he would say, and I would feel a modicum of pride.

For a single line of ten frames, I picked up twenty balls and one hundred pins. In an evening, to earn three dollars, I lifted, threw, and carried close to three tons of balls and pins. On a busy night, with tips, I'd earn four or five dollars, a headache, and bruised shins.

On weekends, I'd go to a movie alone to relax. The films usually began with newsreels -- familiar scenes of B-19s in formation, bomb bay doors open, bombs falling, a line of plumes, puffs of dirt, explosions, or a technological breakthrough, a new bomb site, testing in Nevada; politicians, a historic meeting, Truman, Stalin, and Churchill in deck chairs, smiling, chatting; domestic scenes of factories, steel mills, people in line for nylon stockings, cars at service stations, gasoline rationing, a ship's christening.

I'd be sitting comfortably, chewing Milk Duds, when the scenes would suddenly shift to the Pacific: Marines in battle gear, knee deep in water, weapons held high, wading to a sandy beach bombarded by machine gun and artillery fire. I would begin to shift in my seat as the narrator peppered his narrative with the word "Jap." If the person next to me turned his head ever so slightly, I squirmed. No wonder Papa didn't go to the movies any more.

After a particularly difficult night at the bowling alley, I would brood over our miserable existence. It seemed to me we were losers. The *Issei* with all their talk about inner strength and ancient wisdom hadn't found the dignity they were always talking about. *Gambare*, bear the pain; *shikari-se,* persevere. For what? To live as outcasts? It seemed that Papa and Mama had wasted their lives. Was it supposed to be up to me, the number one son? At five cents a line?

Looking out the window one day after school, I noticed that traffic was slowing down. I assumed there had been an accident and waited to hear sirens. But instead I heard automobile horns and saw a man in a pickup waving his cap in the air. Then he threw it out the window. Traffic had stopped in both directions and the horns kept blowing.

"The war's over, the war's over!" I heard someone shouting loudly. "The Germans have surrendered!" Suddenly people were in the streets celebrating. More than a dozen men and women got out of their cars and buses and embraced outside our window. One man hopped up and down, dancing a jig. Later, I heard the newscast. The war with Germany was over, but I was still afraid to step outside. After all, the war in the Pacific was still being fought.

Papa said Japan would never surrender. He said Japanese soldiers would die before surrendering. I thought that the war would never end. While bombers were bombing Tokyo, I wondered about our relatives. Papa hadn't spoken about them. Was he afraid they were dead? Or was it that he couldn't do anything to help them?

And then, one afternoon in August, the announcement came: Japan had surrendered. I'd witnessed the bomb tests in a theater weeks before -- seen the flash, the power, the churning shaft, the dirt funnel, the cloud, buildings and trucks, like toys under a gigantic mushroom. In Hiroshima after the dust had settled, I saw on film, the remains, emptiness, flatness, grey, somber tones . . . desolation . . . a flat empty landscape . . . nothing, where once a city once stood. . . Hiroshima, the city where Papa was born.

Chapter Eighteen

After we'd been in Denver for several months, Papa received a letter from Rohwer. "It's from *Rokuro*," Papa said to Mama in Japanese.

"I feel badly that he had to write us first," Mama said,

"We were among the last to leave," *Rok-san* wrote. "We tried to help your mother-in-law, but she wouldn't listen. We finally gave up trying. She packed everything herself and left for Stockton without saying goodbye. If she should write, please let us know. We are presently at the Buddhist Church on Pine Street, but should be out soon. The owner of a cleaners near Chinatown just accepted my offer. We are on Pacific Avenue between Taylor and Jones.

"You must be busy. I hope everyone is fine. Maybe it's time for you and your family to return to San Francisco. "

Even before *Rok-san's* letter came, though, Papa had thought of leaving Denver. He was restless. Without any friends in Denver, he drank alone, during and after dinner. He didn't like Denver, he would say. He complained about our unit, the smells in the building, and the lack of heat in the winter, paired with the excessive heat in the summer. He blamed Mrs. *Sakamoto*. But matters got worse when she raised the rent.

"All she does is raise the rent," he said in Japanese while guzzling beer from a bottle. "What does she take us for? I think we should leave." I didn't like our apartment either. I was ready to leave in a heartbeat. I hated carrying our waste water down three flights of stairs.

But now, Papa was more than certain. "We wasting time here," he said, "I tell her we go San Francisco."

"Shouldn't we check the train schedule?" Mama asked in Japanese.

"No," Papa said. "I no like train."

"Why?" Mama asked

"No can sleep on train. Anyway, need car in San Francisco."

Even before Papa decided to return to California, I had been pestering him to give me driving lessons. I was fifteen, then, too young for a learner's permit, but I'd been after him all summer. He said I had to wait until I was sixteen. "But my friends are driving," I'd said. That hadn't mattered to him. I had to be sixteen.

One Sunday afternoon after a picnic at a lake, which we frequented on Sundays, I pestered him again. "My friends didn't need permits. Why should I need one? Why won't you teach me?"

But Papa was in the middle of a discussion with Mama. He ignored me, and said to Mama, "He say I too slow." Papa had been on this topic all afternoon. "I say, 'If I do like you say, you be out of business.' Then he say, 'I boss. You do what I say.'"

Mama sat quietly with *Shii-chan's* head in her lap. They may not have been working at the same place anymore, but Papa still had problems with his boss.

Again, I insisted, "Why won't you teach me how to drive?"

Judging from the expression on his face, I expected him to say in a loud voice, "Motor vehicle no allow . . ." Instead he quietly said, with a slight tremor to his voice, "Okay. I show you. You watch." His tone held a challenge though, implying "You better be ready."

"First like this," he said. I watched intently. Gruffly, he placed his hand over the gear knob and moved it up and down, then side to side. "Now in neutral," he mumbled. When he turned the key, the engine sputtered, coughed, and then purred smoothly.

"This reverse," he said, moving the gear lever to the left and up. "No, no!" he yelled, wide-eyed. He pointed under the dashboard, "No look me! Look down! Look my foot . . . foot on clutch. Clutch very important!"

I leaned over to look. I had a feeling I was in for it now.

"Let out like this . . ." he said, "Then step on gas. See. . . If too much back and forth, push in clutch, like this." His foot went down on the pedal, depressing it to the floor, while the other foot rose off the accelerator. He demonstrated again, but now he was smiling. "Free wheeling like this. . ." He held his arm loosely on the backrest. "When back up . . . turn . . . like this . . ."

We moved backward across the field. The sky glowed pink, and Papa was more at ease with his instructions. "Slow . . . not fast," he said, releasing the pedal slowly while easing on the accelerator. We continued moving backward over a bumpy field, until suddenly I felt like we were falling. I saw the sky momentarily, and then felt the car bounce -- I went up and down, and, with a loud thud, my head slammed into the seat.

"*Waa* . . . ! What happen?" Papa shouted.

We were at an angle. "We're in a ditch or something!" I said. I opened the door and let it swing free. I braced myself on the running board and stepped onto the embankment. Mama and *Shii-chan* pushed open their door and joined me. Papa got out and walked to the back of the car. Looking underneath the car, he said, assuredly, "It okay, only scratch. Universal joint not broken."

He got back inside the car and tried to drive it out of the ditch. But the ground was soft and the rear wheels spun in the mud. "Wait, wait," I yelled. I found some rocks and sticks under a tree and put them in front of the rear tires.

"Okay," I said, and Papa tried again. The wheels only sank deeper. By now it was almost dark. Papa fished out his National Automobile card and told me, "Go store and call tow truck."

I ran to the store and back, worried that the driver of the tow truck might not be able to find us. But while we waited under a tree, I saw the yellow headlights of the truck heading our way. When I waved to the driver, the truck stopped.

"How'd this happen?" he asked Papa, while studying the car. It must have looked strange to see a car angled backwards into a ditch.

"I no know," Papa said, disgustedly. "I backing up and *ga-chan*, it happen. Why they put ditch here?"

"You got me," the driver said. "I think it empties into the lake."

When Papa figured how long it would take to get to California in a car, he decided to teach me how to drive. "Highway driving easy," he said reassuringly, "No need driving permit."

But stick shift wasn't easy as he made it sound. Depressing the accelerator while releasing the clutch was like patting my head and rubbing my stomach simultaneously. My foot on the clutch pedal would shake while the car bucked like a horse . . . jerk, stop . . . jerk, stop . . . jerk, stop.

"No, no!," Papa would yell. "Clutch, clutch, clutch!" When the engine died, he would sigh, "See . . . I told you, clutch! You no step on clutch." But after a week of lessons, I overcame the difficulty. Soon, my stops and starts were flawless, and Papa would say, "You driving very good."

Papa bought a two-wheeled trailer and piled it high with everything we'd accumulated in the year since we left Rohwer: Tables, chairs, a sofa, cabinets, lamps, boxes, suit cases, full of clothes and linens, and spare tires. With the war going on, tires were hard to find, especially for the unusual wheel rim size on the '34 Oldsmobile. Papa bought as many recaps and retreads he could find and placed them on top of the pile and tied ropes over and around everything so that nothing would fall off. The trailer was so heavy that its yoke lifted, slightly, the rear end of the car.

Ping, the mechanic, wired lights for the trailer and checked the engine, transmission, and brakes. "You sure everything okay, Mr. Ping?" asked Papa, "No mechanics in desert, you know."

"Mr. *Omi*, with a cracked block you'll need plenty of water. Better take two water cans to be safe."

Papa also bought a map of the Western States. With a pencil, he drew circles around the landmarks we would head for after leaving Denver. And once we were on the highway he and I would look for signs to take us to where we were headed.

We traveled between 45 and 50 miles an hour on the straightaway, but when the engine shuddered on long climbs, we downshifted to second gear. My driving nearly drove Papa crazy. "*I-yaa* . . . ! More room, more room," he would shout. "Too close, too close! If he stop, you no have time. Trailer heavy, take time to stop car!"

During a long uphill climb, I'd keep my eye on the temperature gauge. If the needle began to move into the red, I'd stop and let the engine cool. Sometimes, I'd try for the top of the hill, and if I made it, I'd coast downhill to cool the engine. But if steam began hissing out from under the cowling near the radiator cap, I'd pull over to heed

Papa's warning. "If you no stop, piston freeze, then engine no more good."

After I'd turned off the engine, Papa would unlatch the cowling and wait for the bubbling sounds to stop. "I make big mistake," he would grumble, "Never buy car in Denver." When he thought the engine had cooled, he would wrap a towel around the radiator cap, slowly unscrew it, and wave me away with a sweep of his arm. "Too danger," he would tell me. The radiator would hiss like a tea kettle, and suddenly hot water would bubble out of the spout. Papa would turn his head and leap away like a frog. When the car overheated near a filling station, I felt relieved that I could use a hose instead of a watering can.

We'd pull into the service station like a locomotive: steam pouring out of the radiator. While I uncoiled the hose, Papa would unlatch the cowling. I'd aim the hose on the honeycomb part of the radiator and drench it until the engine cooled. As we drove off, I was embarrassed about the large puddle of water I'd left near the gas pump.

While we were driving through Wyoming and Utah, I often stopped at different farmhouses for water. I never knew what to expect. Sometimes the person who came to the door would have very little to say. They'd point to a well or a hose to let me know I could have their water. Of course, I was grateful and thanked them profusely.

"Good afternoon," I said one day, "I was wondering if you could let me have some water for our car." I held up the watering can for her to see.

"For heav'n sakes, young man, where's your car at?

"Over there." I pointed. She shaded her eyes and nodded.

"Of course you can. Where you headed?"

"California, ma'am."

"That's a long way."

"Yes, ma'am."

"Is that your family outside the car?"

"Yes ma'am, my father, mother, and sister."

"I just baked some pie. Would you and your family like some?"

The pie smelled good, but I knew Papa would say no. He was too proud. And I couldn't go inside to eat while they were waiting. "Thank you ma'am, but I'll just have the water, if it's all right with you."

Sometimes, no one was at home -- at least, it appeared that way. I'd scoop water out of a trough or hoist water out of a well, while looking to see if anyone was watching. That was when I felt like a thief.

We drove for miles and miles, filling the radiator with water and changing tires. But outside Winnemucca, Nevada, in the middle of the afternoon, we ran out of tires. While Mama and *Shii-chan* sat on the running board on the shady side of the car, Papa and I looked for help from a passerby. But there were very few cars on the road that day. Whenever we saw a car coming toward us, Papa and I would wave our arms and watch it slow down as it drew closer. Just when we thought it would stop, it only slowed down momentarily. Suddenly it would speed away. Sometimes I would hold out my thumb, instead of waving my arms, but it didn't matter. Drivers and passengers pretended not to see us. They looked straight ahead and sped past us as though we weren't there.

Finally, Papa and I untied the bike and lifted it off the trailer. Though the handlebar was hot to touch, the rubber handles were not. While straddling the bike, I listened to Papa's instructions. I could feel heat rising through the soles of my shoes. "Find garage," he said. "You say we no have no more spare tire. And no can fix recap. You ask how best way to California. Train or bus? You speaking better me. That's why, I no go." He gave me two ten-dollar bills. "You say you Papa sell car cheap."

I peddled along the shoulder of the highway, avoiding ruts and potholes. Power poles and sagging wires rippled through the shimmering asphalt. After a few miles, I saw a pickup truck coming toward me. I coasted to a stop and waited for it to go by, but it slowed down and stopped. "What in the hell you doing out here on a bicycle?" the man asked me. When I told him about our car, he lifted his baseball cap and scratched his red hair. His face was covered with freckles. Without another word, he loaded my bike into the back of his truck and drove me back to our car.

"No more spare tire," Papa told him. "You want to buy? Only need tire. Very good condition. I sell cheap."

"No, mister," the man said, "But I think I know where we might find you a tire." Papa and the man drove away and returned awhile later with a recapped tire. "We very lucky." Papa said to Mama and me with a smile on his face. "He find tire."

The man helped Papa change the tire and when Papa tried to pay him, he refused. Papa put two ten dollar bills into the man's shirt pocket. "Please, you take. You very nice man. I no know what we do if you no help."

"Thanks mister," the man said with a smile, "And good luck in California."

I was driving when we got to the Sierra Nevada mountains. As we descended a long gentle grade, I downshifted to second gear and pumped the brake pedal like Papa had said I should. "No keep foot on brake all the time," he had said." Brakes wear out." But each time I pumped the pedal, though I pushed down hard, the car kept going faster. When I felt it swerve one way and then the other, I could see the trailer swaying in the rear view mirror. I struggled to keep the car in the lane. A slight adjustment of the wheel in the opposite direction offset the swaying. But I began to feel the trailer tug more strongly. Gripping the steering wheel tightly, I turned it only slightly right or left to compensate for the whipping action. Fortunately, the road was nearly straight, but we were picking up speed.

"Brake! Brake!" Papa yelled.

I found the emergency brake with my left hand and pulled it up several notches, but it wasn't enough. Up ahead, I saw a stop sign. My foot was all the way down on the brake pedal and the emergency brake was all the way back. We flew through the intersection past a blur of cars and people. Eventually, the road leveled out and the car gradually slowed down. Finally, we stopped.

Papa stammered "*Osoroshi kata. Mo, minna ga shinu to omota.* I thought we all were going to die!" Mama and *Shii-chan* were speechless.

Papa drove the car to a service station and had the brakes adjusted. Then he drove the rest of the way to Sacramento, where we stopped for sandwiches and lemonade. The warm air of the valley lulled me to sleep until Papa shouted, "Look, look! Bay Bridge! Bay Bridge! We here!"

"Bay Bridge! Bay Bridge!" *Shii-chan* squealed. We were on the highway near Emeryville and the tide was out. A cool breeze wafted a familiar odor of rotten eggs into our car. Nothing had changed. I gazed at the bridge, its looping cables, the white caps on the water, the city, the hills rising behind it. At last, the hills, they stirred my heart. Nowhere else could we be but San Francisco. We'd made it back . . . we were home, home at last.

Chapter Nineteen

We finally made it to *Rok-san's* cleaners on Pacific Avenue, tired and hungry. We wore the clothes we wore last night and had slept somewhere in Nevada. We all needed a bath, and Papa needed a shave. With large circles under his eyes, Papa pushed open the door and a bell tinkled. *Rok-san* looked up from his press machine. His eyes changed from wonderment to a smile. He welcomed us in with a whiskbroom. *Obasan,* who had been sewing a garment, stood up next to the sewing machine, and said, "*M-a-a-a,* its nice to see you," in a cheery voice, "Come in, come in." And suddenly, the tiredness disappeared. I felt ready for a snack.

"You have a nice place," Mama said to *Obasan.*

"Its nothing, really, " She replied cheerfully, "But we had to get out of that church gymnasium. The people were nice but we had no privacy. *Takashi* couldn't keep still."

Their cleaners looked neat and tidy: no half-opened cardboard boxes or cartons in sight. Everything had been put away. But unlike their cleaners before the War, this place looked bleak. The ceilings and walls looked old and the linoleum on the floor was worn. *Obasan* took us in back to the living room and kitchen.

Takashi's room had newly flowered wallpaper and children's furniture. Shelves were lined with toys and stuffed animals. Everything looked orderly and new, but nothing looked played with. "He has his own room," *Shii-chan* whispered. "Isn't he lucky? *Obasan* must buy him everything. And I thought, so many toys that he can't play with them all.

"He's such a good boy," *Obasan* said when she saw us staring. "He'll be five in November. He reminds me of you when you were little, *Minoru-chan*. He loves funny books the way you did." His books were also neatly stacked.

"Where is he?" I asked. I wondered what he looked like.

"He's with the Chinese boy next door," *Obasan* said. "They play together all the time.

"He's starting kindergarten next year," *Rok-san* said. "It's the same school you and *Shii-chan* went to when you were on Polk Street."

The words Polk Street brought back so many memories. I wondered if Mr. Goldberg was still there. Maybe we could eat breakfast in his diner and see the butterflies in his yard. I wondered whether the Murphy bed was still there in the wall.

Though we'd only been away for three years, I felt the way Rip Van Winkle must have felt. The changes were startling. The hills near Chinatown seemed steeper and the streets, narrower. And when we drove past my elementary school, its yard felt smaller and hemmed in between buildings. The cable car tracks I used to nimbly cross seemed narrower, smoother and, shinier. Familiar places seemed strange. So many new stores and signs. But I'd changed also. Mama said I had grown at least a foot taller in the last year. I was now several inches taller than Papa, and my voice had gone from soprano to bass.

After *Obasan's* snack, *Rok-san* invited us to stay overnight, but Papa said no. He was afraid to leave our trailer in the street. *Rok-san* offered to cover it with canvas, but Papa said that we had to find our own place.

We left *Rok-san's* cleaners before dark, pulling the trailer behind us. Sometimes I could smell burning rubber when Papa held the car on a hill with his clutch, waiting for the signal to change. Mama wanted to stay at a hotel, but Papa said, "No, too expensive." He circled Japanese Town, went up Post Street, down Laguna, past Sutter and Bush, down Pine Street, until finally, on the comer of Pine and Buchanan, he saw a sign in an apartment window that said, "For Rent".

"We lucky," he said, backing the car up to the curb. In the entrance alcove of the basement unit, Papa rang the bell. Papa pushed the button several more times, and then said, "Maybe somebody upstairs." So we walked around the comer to the unit upstairs, and Papa rapped on a wooden door.

"Hold on there," a voice from inside said. A large black woman stuck her head outside the door.

"You owner?" Papa said.

"Yes, I am. Is there a problem, mister?" she said with a cold stare.

"I see sign. Can I rent?"

"Sure thing," she said. This time she smiled. "Rent's twenty-five a month, including utilities. I'll need the first month's rent now and twenty-five the first day of every month. The room in back's already rented, so you'll have to share the kitchen and bathroom with him. His name is Jefferson."

"Okay, we take," Papa said, fishing a twenty and a five out of his wallet. The lady gave Papa a key to the unit and we went back to the car.

Mr. Jefferson must have heard us moving in because he shuffled into the living room with a smile. He was a tall, hefty man, six feet at least, in a neat, well-pressed, three-piece suit. But he moved slowly with his back bent, using a white cane, squinting through thick glasses.

Mama was horrified. "How could you even consider this place," she whispered to Papa in Japanese. "I don't want to live with a *kurombo!*" she exclaimed, using the Japanese slang for "black person."

Papa whispered that the apartment was well located since Japanese town was only two blocks away. Mama didn't argue because Papa had already made up his mind. But Japanese Town was not the Japanese Town of old. *Kurombos* and Filipinos had moved into the area. Still, Japanese families who hadn't sold their property became the core. Grocery, hardware, dry goods, clothing, furniture, radio and appliance stores gradually began to appear again along Post, Webster, Laguna, Octavia, Bush, Pine and Buchanan Streets, as did barbershops, drugstores, coffee shops and soda fountains.

And that was our new beginning after the war. Whether it be age, maturity, the times, not only had our surrounds changed, but we had changed as well. And this after only three years. It was much like the tale of *Urashimataro*, the story of a boy who returned from an enchanted island, a paradise island, where he was given a box as a gift and told never to open it. But it was irresistible, like the Apple from the Garden of Eden, and *Urashimataro* couldn't help opening the box. And when he did, he was engulfed in a mystical cloud and suddenly transformed into a shriveled old man. Had I opened the same box, the cloud would have engulfed everything but me. Everything had changed but me.

I had wanted so much to return to the pre-War days, but I was alone. Papa and Mama focused on regaining what had been taken away. They returned to the dry cleaning business and *Shii-chan* and I helped. Everyone else was too busy to care. We were not the family I grew up with. No more picnics and family gatherings. Our close-knit lives had unraveled like a wool sweater. All that was left was the yarn: Papa, Mama, *Shii-chan* and me. We pulled together to get our lives back on track. *Rok-san* and *Obasan, Ojii-san, Obaa-san*, Uncle Ken, Uncle *Kazuo*, Henry, George, Amy, Ben, and our relatives in Japan were no longer connected the way they had been before the war. I would often wonder, had there not been a war, would our lives have been any different? After the war, we all pursued new and different ventures, keeping up with payments on homes and automobiles and raising children like everyone else in America.

In 1953, with the passage of the McCarren Walters Act, Papa and Mama became naturalized citizens. *Shii-chan* and I transferred title to the house they bought in our names in 1949. This was their very first house. They had finally realized their American dream.

CPSIA information can be obtained at www.ICGtesting.com
Printed in the USA
LVOW08s0158041016

507278LV00001B/150/P